JONES & BARTLETT LEARNING INFORMATION SYSTEMS SECURITY

LABORATORY MANUAL TO ACCOMPANY

Network Security, Firewalls, and VPNs

1E REVISED

virtualsecurity CLOUD labs
powered by TOOLWIRE

VLAB SOLUTIONS

JONES & BARTLETT
LEARNING

World Headquarters
Jones & Bartlett Learning
5 Wall Street
Burlington, MA 01803
978-443-5000
info@jblearning.com
www.jblearning.com

Jones & Bartlett Learning books and products are available through most bookstores and online booksellers. To contact Jones & Bartlett Learning directly, call 800-832-0034, fax 978-443-8000, or visit our website, www.jblearning.com.

Substantial discounts on bulk quantities of Jones & Bartlett Learning publications are available to corporations, professional associations, and other qualified organizations. For details and specific discount information, contact the special sales department at Jones & Bartlett Learning via the above contact information or send an email to specialsales@jblearning.com.

Production Credits
Chief Executive Officer: Ty Field
President: James Homer
SVP, Editor-in-Chief: Michael Johnson
SVP, Chief Marketing Officer: Alison M. Pendergast
SVP, Curriculum Solutions: Christopher Will
Director of Sales, Curriculum Solutions: Randi Roger
Author: vLab Solutions, LLC, David Kim, President
Editorial Management: High Stakes Writing, LLC, Lawrence J. Goodrich, Editor and Publisher
Copy Editor, High Stakes Writing: Katherine Dillin
Copy Editor, High Stakes Writing: Ruth Walker
Senior Editorial Assistant: Rainna Erikson
Reprints and Special Projects Manager: Susan Schultz
Associate Production Editor: Tina Chen
Rights & Photo Research Associate: Lian Bruno
Manufacturing and Inventory Control Supervisor: Amy Bacus
Senior Marketing Manager: Andrea DeFronzo
Cover Design: Anne Spencer
Composition: CAE Solutions Corp.
Cover Image: © ErickN/ShutterStock, Inc.
Printing and Binding: Edwards Brothers Malloy
Cover Printing: Edwards Brothers Malloy

ISBN: 978-1-4496-3850-4

6048
Printed in the United States of America
16 15 14 13 12 10 9 8 7 6 5 4 3

Contents

Ethics and Code of Conduct

The material presented in this course is designed to give you a real-life look at the use of various tools and systems that are at the heart of every network security analyst's daily responsibilities. Through use of this material, you will have access to software and techniques used every day by professionals. With this access come certain ethical responsibilities.

The hardware, software, tools, and applications presented and used in this lab manual and/or the VSCL are intended to be used for instructional and educational purposes only.

As a student in this course, you are not to use these tools, applications, or techniques on live production IT infrastructures inside or outside of your campus or organization. Under no circumstances are you permitted to use these tools, applications, or techniques on the production IT infrastructures and networks of other organizations.

You are required to conform to your school or organization's Code of Conduct and ethics policies during the use of this lab manual and any of the tools, applications, or techniques described within.

Preface

Welcome! This lab manual is your step-by-step guide to completing the laboratory exercises for this course.

Virtual Security Cloud Lab (VSCL)

For most of the exercises in this lab manual, you will use the Virtual Security Cloud Lab (VSCL) resource.

> **Note:**
> The Virtual Security Cloud Lab requires use of either **Windows Internet Explorer** or **Mozilla Firefox**. The Virtual Security Cloud Lab does not support Google Chrome, Safari, or Opera at this time.

The VSCL is a collection of virtual resources, including Windows and Linux servers, Cisco routers, and applications such as Wireshark, FileZilla, and Nessus®, that will allow you to perform all of the tasks in this lab manual as if you were performing them in a live production environment. The heart of the VSCL is a Windows Workstation desktop configured to give you access to the tools and resources you need for each lab, without any special setup on your part.

As noted in the following table, some of the exercises in this lab manual will be performed without using the VSCL. For detailed instructions on how to perform these exercises, please consult your syllabus or instructor.

How to Use This Lab Manual

This lab manual features step-by-step instructions for completing the following hands-on lab exercises:

VSCL	LAB TITLE
Yes	Lab #1: Analyze Essential TCP/IP Networking Protocols
Yes	Lab #2: Network Documentation
Yes	Lab #3: Network Discovery and Reconnaissance Probing Using Zenmap GUI (Nmap)
Yes	Lab #4: Perform a Software Vulnerability Scan and Assessment with Nessus®
Yes	Lab #5: Configure a Microsoft® Windows Workstation Internal IP Stateful Firewall
No	Lab #6: Design a De-Militarized Zone (DMZ) for a LAN-to-WAN Ingress/Egress
Yes	Lab #7: Implement a VPN Tunnel Between a Microsoft® Server and Microsoft® Client
No	Lab #8: Design a Layered Security Strategy for an IP Network Infrastructure
Yes	Lab #9: Construct a Linux Host Firewall and Monitor for IP Traffic
Yes	Lab #10: Design and Implement Security Operations Management Best Practices

Video Walkthroughs of Each Lab

Each VSCL-based exercise in this lab manual includes a video walkthrough that gives you a quick overview of every step and function. You can watch the video walkthrough prior to performing the lab exercise, and refer to it as necessary while you complete the lab. You can pause, rewind, and fast-forward the video walkthroughs if you need to take notes or spend extra time on a particular step or function. Consult your syllabus or instructor for information on where to locate the walkthrough videos.

Step-by-Step Instructions

You'll find it easy to complete these lab exercises by following the detailed step-by-step instructions. Each step is clearly broken down into sub-steps, and all actions you are required to take are noted in **bold** font. Screenshots are included to help you identify key menus, dialog boxes, and input locations. If you get stuck on a step, refer to the lab video, which follows the order of the steps.

Deliverables

At the completion of each lab, you'll be asked to provide a set of deliverables to your instructor. These deliverables may include documents, files, screenshots, and/or answers to assessment questions. The deliverables are designed to test your understanding of the information, and your successful completion of the lab's steps and functions. For specific information on deliverables, refer to the **Deliverables** section in each lab.

> **Note:**
> Some labs require the use of a word processor (such as Microsoft® Word) for preparing and submitting deliverables. If you do not have access to a word processor, you can use OpenOffice v3.3 on the Workstation desktop of the VSCL to prepare your documents. It includes a word processor called Writer that has all the features necessary for creating documents for use in these labs.

File Transfer

At times, you may be asked to transfer files that you've created while performing lab steps in the VSCL to another computer. You can do this using the File Transfer function built into the VSCL's vWorkstation desktop. Instructions for preparing and sending files using the File Transfer function can be found at the beginning of the video walkthrough for the first lab in each course (in most cases, Lab #1).

> **Note:**
> Use of this lab manual or the VSCL **does not require use of the textbook**. If you have questions about whether a textbook is needed for your course, consult your instructor.

Analyze Essential TCP/IP Networking Protocols

LAB 1

Introduction

In this lab, you will learn how to use a protocol analyzer to capture and analyze IP packets. Understanding how to distinguish proper from improper protocol behavior is a key skill for most network security analysts. Using the Wireshark protocol analyzer tool (sometimes called a "packet sniffer"), you'll capture IP traffic from a variety of sources and use that data to identify and become familiar with the common network protocols used in a typical network infrastructure.

Learning Objectives

Upon completing this lab, you will be able to:

- Use Wireshark protocol analyzer as a packet capture and protocol analysis tool
- Capture and decode ARP, DHCP, ICMP, TCP, and UDP traffic
- Capture and decode Telnet, FTP, and SSH sessions and identify SEQ and ACK numbers
- Distinguish between proper and improper protocol behavior, that is, TCP three-way handshake, cleartext vs. ciphertext
- Identify common network-related protocols used for client-server communications, network management, and network security

TOOLS AND SOFTWARE USED

NAME	MORE INFORMATION
Wireshark	http://www.wireshark.org/
PuTTY	http://www.chiark.greenend.org.uk/~sgtatham/putty/
FileZilla Server and FileZilla Client	http://filezilla-project.org/
Tftpd32	http://tftpd32.jounin.net/
RSA NetWitness Investigator	http://www.emc.com/security/rsa-netwitness.htm

Deliverables

Upon completion of this lab, you are required to provide the following deliverables to your instructor:

1. A copy of your Wireshark Lab #1.pcap file in electronic format;
2. A screen capture of your successful NetWitness Investigator packet capture import, as a text document;
3. Lab Assessment Questions & Answers for Lab #1.

Hands-On Steps

1. This lab begins at the student landing vWorkstation virtual machine desktop of the VSCL, as shown here.

FIGURE 1.1

"Student Landing" VSCL workstation

2. To start the Wireshark application, **double-click** on the **Wireshark icon** on the desktop.
3. When the Wireshark window appears, **click** the **Citrix Systems link** in the area marked "Interface List." This tells Wireshark which interface to monitor for activity. In this case, you are capturing data from the virtual environment. In a production environment, you would see a list of interfaces corresponding to the resources available in that environment (servers, nodes, etc.).

FIGURE 1.2

The Wireshark window

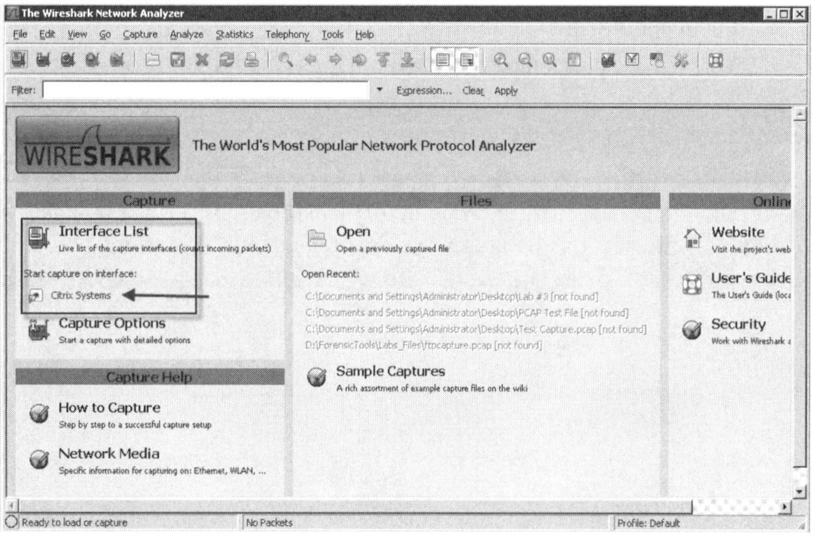

Once you select Citrix Systems, Wireshark begins capturing data, which you will see as lines of information in the application window.

4. **Minimize** the **Wireshark application window**.
5. Start the Windows Command Prompt by **clicking Start > Run** and **typing cmd** in the dialog box.

> **Note:**
> To collect data for analysis, Wireshark must have a stream of incoming packets to capture. The next steps cover how to feed IP packets to Wireshark using ping, Telnet, and Secure Shell (SSH) connections. These connections generate packets on the virtual environment interface, which are then captured by Wireshark.

6. From the Windows Command Prompt application window, **type ping 172.30.0.8** and **press Enter**. Note the Reply responses, which indicate the two-way passage of packets.

FIGURE 1.3

Windows Command Prompt

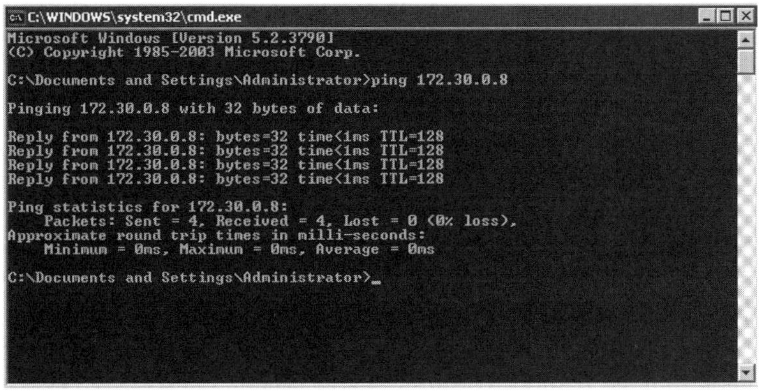

7. Next, **type ping 172.30.0.200** and **press Enter**. Note again the Reply responses. **Minimize** the **Windows Command Prompt window**.

   You've now created a packet stream for Wireshark.

> **Note:**
> PuTTY is a terminal emulator program that you can use as a client to create a variety of secure connections to network resources. This lab uses it to create Telnet and SSH sessions.

8. **Double-click** the **PuTTY icon** on the desktop to start the PuTTY application.
9. In the PuTTY application window, **type** the IP address for LAN Switch 1, **172.16.8.5**. **Select** the **Telnet radio button** and **click** the **Open button**.

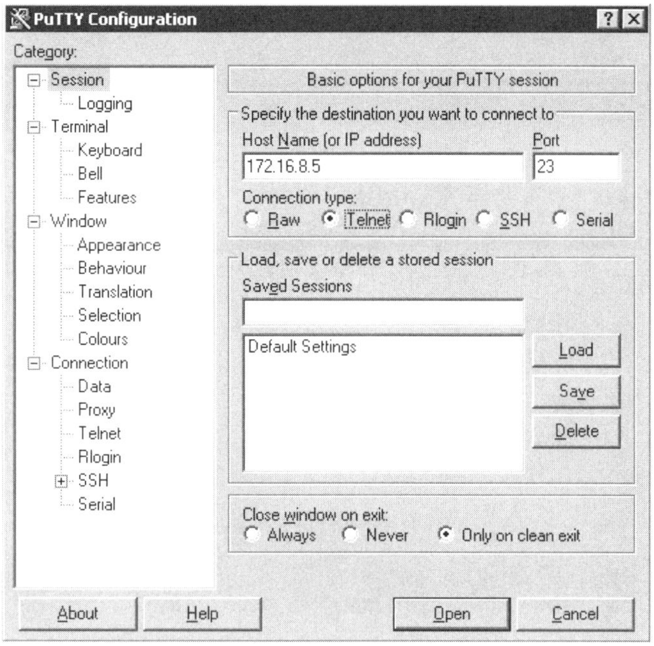

FIGURE 1.4
PuTTY application window

10. PuTTY will launch a terminal console window. At the login prompt, type the following:
    - Username: **cisco**
    - Password: **cisco**

FIGURE 1.5
PuTTY terminal console window

You have now established a Telnet connection to LAN Switch 1, sending more packets to Wireshark. **Type quit** to close the terminal console window.

11. **Double-click** the **PuTTY icon** to restart the application. This time, in the PuTTY application window, **type** the IP address for LAN Switch 2, **172.16.20.5**, **select** the **SSH radio button** and **click** the **Open button** to start the connection.
12. You will see another terminal console window. **Type** the username **cisco** and the password **cisco** at the login prompt to establish the SSH connection. **Type quit** at the command line to close the terminal console window.

> **Note:**
> The next steps involve using the File Transfer Protocol (FTP) to send files to and from client and server computers so that Wireshark can capture packet data from larger, more complex traffic. You'll be using the vWorkstation desktop, a virtual Windows server, and the FileZilla and Tftpd32 applications to accomplish this.

13. **Double-click** on the **ISSA_VM Server Farm_RDP folder** on the desktop to open it. Start the virtual Windows server connection by **double-clicking** on the **TargetWindows01.RDP icon**.
14. **Log onto** the **TargetWindows01 virtual server** using the following credentials:
    - Username: **Administrator**
    - Password: **ISS316Security**

> **Note:**
> Passwords are case sensitive. Type them exactly as you see them.

The virtual server desktop will load when you are logged on.

15. The FileZilla server application starts automatically when the server starts. **Click OK** when you see the Connect to Server dialog box to open a connection with the FileZilla FTP server interface.

FIGURE 1.6

Connect to Server dialog box

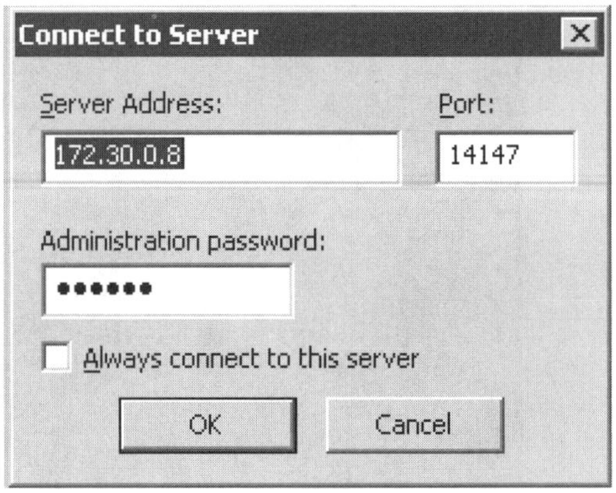

16. **Minimize** the **virtual server desktop** and return to the vWorkstation desktop.
17. **Double-click** the **FileZilla icon** on the desktop to start the FileZilla client application. When the window launches, enter the following logon credentials:

    - Host: **172.30.0.8**
    - Username: **student**
    - Password: **ISS316Security**
    - Port: **21**

FIGURE 1.7
FileZilla client application

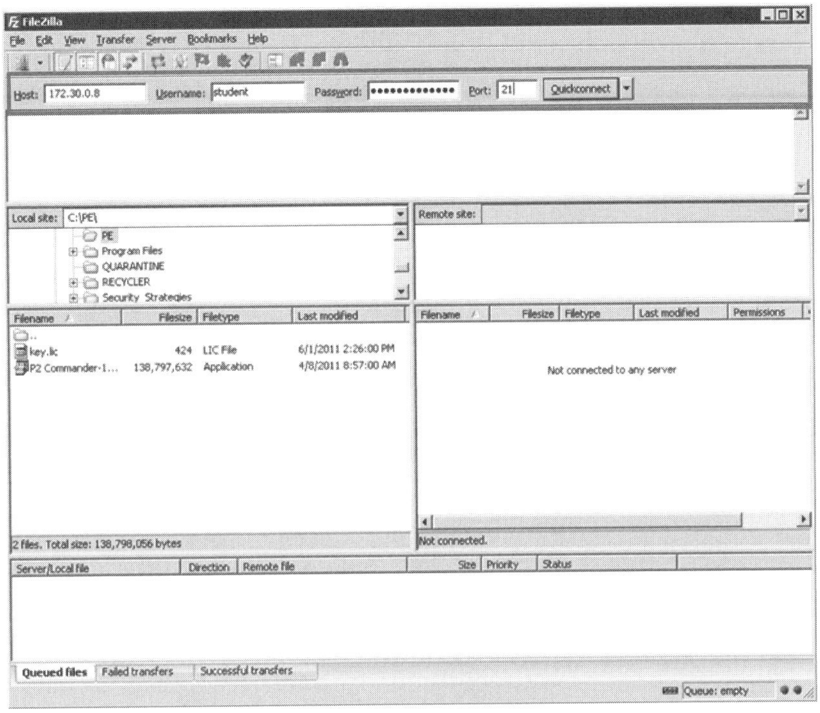

18. **Click** the **Quickconnect button** to log onto the FTP server.

19. FTP a file from FileZilla client to FileZilla server by doing the following:
   a. From the local site (left-hand pane), **double-click** the **ISSA_TOOLS folder** to open it (you may have to scroll to find it), then **double-click** on the **Documentation folder**
   b. **Highlight** the **AnyConnect_adminguide.pdf file** and **drag** it to the remote site root drive (**C:**) in the right-hand pane

FIGURE 1.8

FTP a file from FileZilla client to FileZilla server

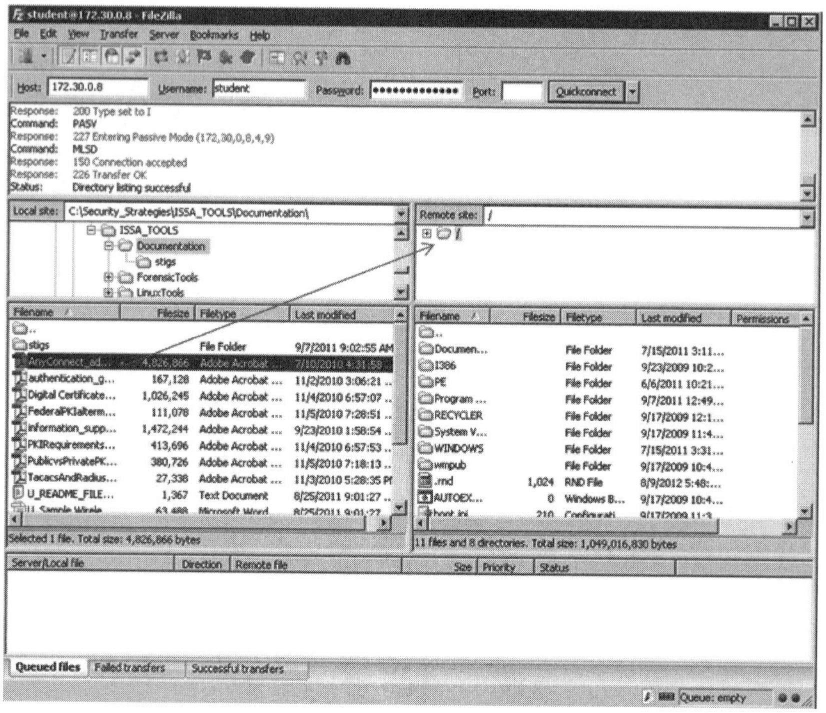

20. Verify that you have placed the file in the correct drive on the remote site by doing the following:
   a. **Maximize** the **virtual Windows server window**
   b. **Double-click** the **My Computer icon** on the server desktop and **look for** the **AnyConnect_adminguide.pdf file** there
21. **Close** the **FileZilla server window** on the virtual server.
22. **Double-click** on the **Tftpd32_SE Admin icon** on the desktop to start the Tftpd32 application.
23. When the application window launches, **click** the **Tftp Client tab** to set up the TargetWindows01 virtual server as the Tftp client.

FIGURE 1.9

The Tftp Client tab

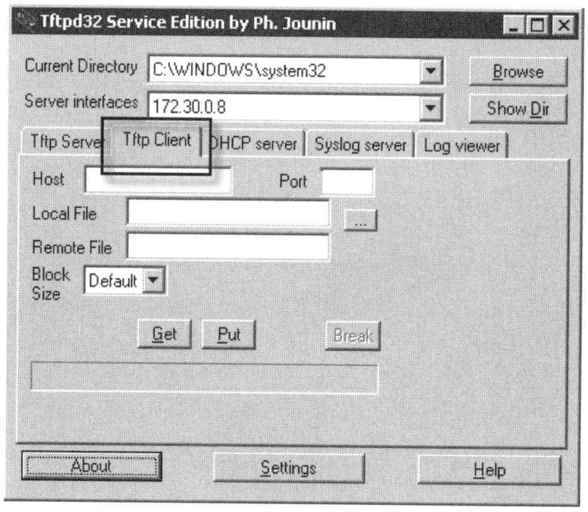

24. **Switch back to** the **vWorkstation desktop, close the FileZilla client application,** and **double-click** the **Tftpd32_SE Admin icon** on the desktop to start the Tftpd32 application.
25. When the application window launches, **click** the **Tftp Server tab** to set up your vWorkstation as the Tftp server.

FIGURE 1.10

The Tftp Server tab

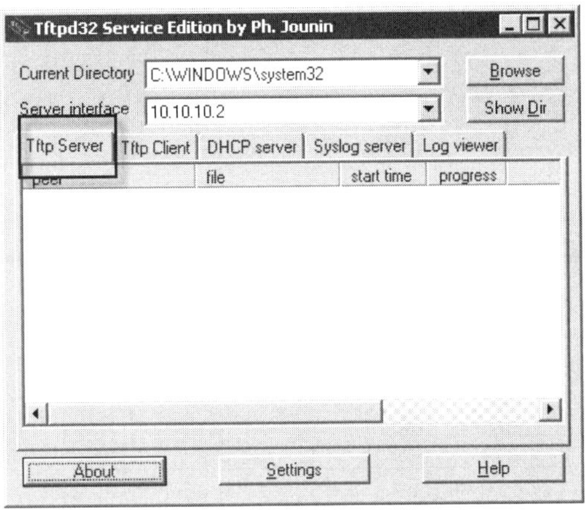

26. **Switch back to** the **TargetWindows01 virtual server** and **enter** the following connection information:
    - Host: **172.30.0.2**
    - Port: **69**
    - Local file: **C:\AnyConnect_adminguide.pdf**

Note:
This is the file you previously sent to the TargetWindows01 virtual server's root drive using FileZilla.

27. **Click** the **Put button** to start the FTP file transfer. You've just transferred the file from the virtual server to the vWorkstation; Wireshark captured those packets.

FIGURE 1.11

Click the Put button

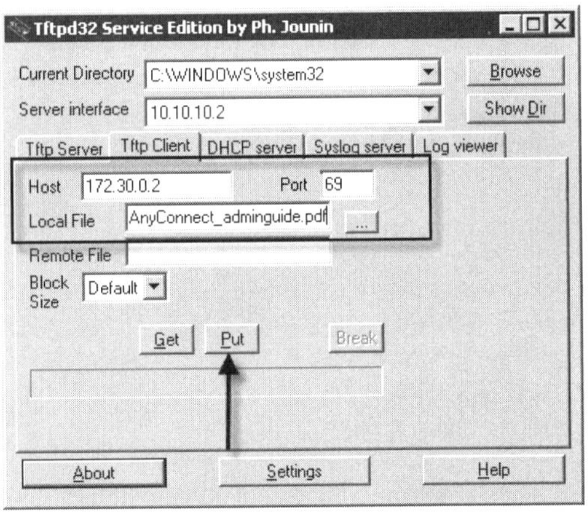

28. **Close** the **Tftpd32 application** on the TargetWindows01 server, and **switch back to** the **vWorkstation**. **Close** the **Tftpd32 application** on the vWorkstation.

29. **Maximize** the **Wireshark application window** from the vWorkstation application tray.
30. **Click** the **Stop the running live capture icon** to stop the packet capture process.
31. **Review** the packet capture data in the Wireshark window, paying close attention to the "Protocol" and "Info" columns. **Identify** the protocols and events related to the steps you just performed.

FIGURE 1.12

Packet capture data in the Wireshark window

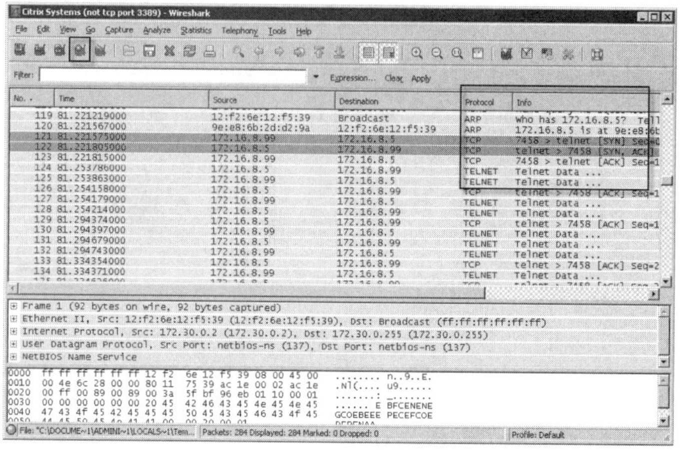

> **Note:**
>
> It is useful to sort the Wireshark data by columns, particularly by the "Protocol" column, which will give you a good understanding of which protocols (TCP, Telnet, FTP, etc.) are attached to which events. To sort by columns, click on the **column header**.

32. **Click** the **Save icon** to save the packet capture. When the Wireshark: Save file as dialog box opens, **name** the file **Lab #1** and **select Wireshark/tcpdump...libpcap [*.pcap, *.cap]** from the "Save as type" menu. **Save** the file to the Security_Strategies folder (**My Computer > Local Disk (C:) > Security_Strategies**).

FIGURE 1.13

Wireshark: Save file as dialog box

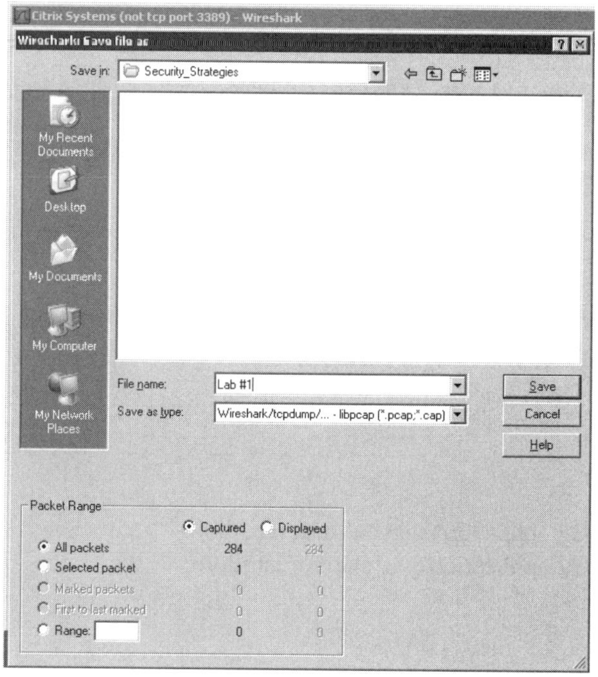

33. **Download** the **Lab #1.pcap file** to your local computer using the File Transfer button on the vWorkstation desktop and **submit** it as part of your deliverables. (If you need help using the File Transfer tool, there is a detailed explanation at the beginning of the video walkthrough for this lab exercise.)

> **Note:**
> The next steps will show you how to use RSA NetWitness Investigator to analyze the Wireshark packet capture. NetWitness Investigator allows you to look at and analyze packet capture data in context, so that you are able to act on any threats or problems quickly and easily. These steps show you how to build a NetWitness Investigator local collection, which you can use to analyze and submit your package capture data to your instructor as part of the lab deliverables.

34. **Double-click** the **NetWitness Investigator icon** on the vWorkstation desktop to start the application.
35. When the application window launches, **click Collection** in the toolbar and **select New Local Collection** from the drop-down menu.
36. In the New Local Collection dialog box, **name** the collection **Lab #1** and save it to the default location by **clicking OK**.

FIGURE 1.14

New Local Collection dialog box

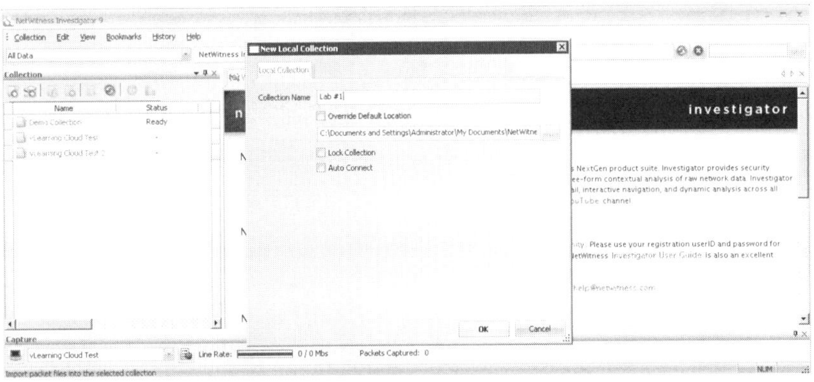

37. **Double-click** on the **Lab #1 folder** that appears in the left-hand Collection pane to **set** it to **Ready**.
38. **Click** the **Import Packets icon** from the menu.
39. In the pop-up window, **navigate** to the Security_Strategies folder (**My Computer** > **Local Disk (C:)** > **Security_Strategies**) and **select** the **Lab #1.pcap file**. **Click Open** to import the file.

FIGURE 1.15

The Security_Strategies folder

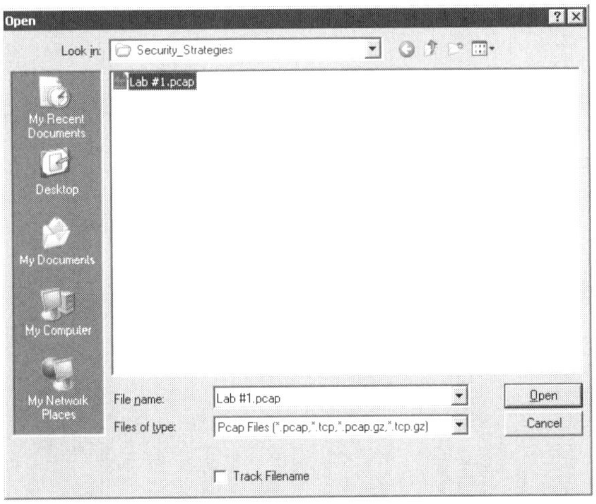

40. **Double-click** the **Lab #1 folder** to open the collection. **Review** the summary information, identifying the following:
    - Service and protocol types
    - Source and destination IP addresses
    - Host aliases detected
    - TCP three-way handshake
    - SEQ#, ACK#, IP data payload
    - ARP, DHCP, ICMP
    - FTP, TFTP, Telnet, and SSH
41. When the import is finished, **make a screen capture** of the **NetWitness screen** and **paste** it into a text document. **Submit** it to your instructor as a deliverable.

> **Note:**
> To capture the screen, **press** the **Ctrl** and **PrtSc** keys together, and then **use Ctrl + V** to paste the image into a Word or other word processor document.

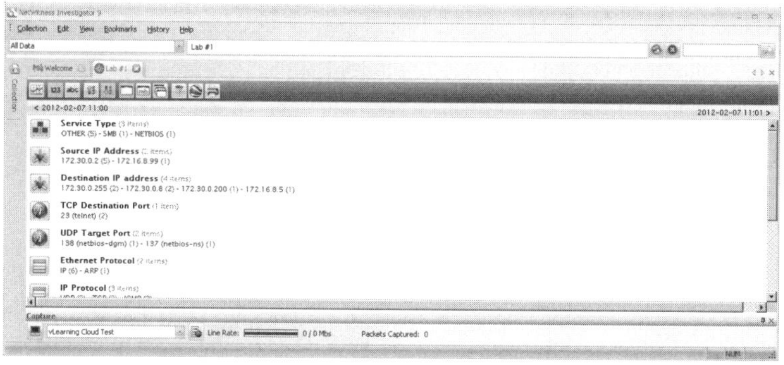

FIGURE 1.16
Summary information

Evaluation Criteria and Rubrics

The following are the evaluation criteria and rubrics for Lab #1 that students must perform:

1. Was the student able to use Wireshark protocol analyzer as a packet capture and protocol analysis tool? – [**20%**]
2. Was the student able to capture and decode ARP, DHCP, ICMP, TCP, and UDP traffic? – [**20%**]
3. Was the student able to capture and decode Telnet, FTP, and SSH sessions and identify SEQ and ACK numbers? – [**20%**]
4. Was the student able to distinguish between proper and improper protocol behavior, that is, TCP three-way handshake, cleartext vs. ciphertext? – [**20%**]
5. Was the student able to identify common network-related protocols used for client-server communications, network management, and network security? – [**20%**]

LAB #1 – ASSESSMENT WORKSHEET

Analyze Essential TCP/IP Networking Protocols

Course Name and Number: ______________________________

Student Name: ______________________________

Instructor Name: ______________________________

Lab Due Date: ______________________________

Overview

One of the most important tools for information systems security practitioners is a packet capture and protocol analysis tool. Wireshark is a freeware tool providing basic packet capture and protocol decoding capabilities. NetWitness Investigator is a free and commercial solution (the free version allows up to 20 1GB collections of packet captures) that provides security practitioners with a deep packet inspection tool for examining everything from the data link layer up to the application layer. NetWitness Investigator is the only protocol analysis tool that provides deep packet inspection and advanced decoding for simplified full packet capture and session analysis.

Lab Assessment Questions & Answers

1. What is the purpose of the address resolution protocol (ARP)?

____

____

____

____

2. What is the purpose of the dynamic host control protocol (DHCP)?

____

____

____

____

3. Identify the DHCP allocated source IP host address for the vWorkstation desktop and the TargetWindows01 virtual server.

4. When you pinged the targeted IP host (172.30.0.8 or 172.30.0.200), what was the source IP address and destination IP address of the ICMP echo-request packet?

5. Did the targeted IP host respond to the ICMP echo-request packet with an ICMP echo-reply packet? If yes, how many ICMP echo-request packets were sent back to the IP source?

6. Find a TCP three-way handshake for a Telnet, FTP, or SSH session. What is the significance of the TCP three-way handshake?

7. What was the SEQ# of the initial SYN TCP packet and ACK# of the SYN ACK TCP packet?

8. During the instructor's Telnet session to LAN Switch 1 and LAN Switch 2, what was the captured terminal password for LAN Switch 1 and LAN Switch 2?

9. When the instructor used SSH to a Cisco router, were you able to see the terminal password? Why or why not?

10. What other IP packets are on the VLAN and Ethernet LAN segment? How can these other IP packets provide additional clues or information about the logical IP routing and IP addressing schema?

Network Documentation

LAB 2

Introduction

In this lab, you will learn how to use several different applications and interfaces to identify and document an IP network design and schema. Chief among these is PuTTY, which you used in Lab #1. The primary use of PuTTY is to establish Telnet and SSH sessions to remote servers. You will use PuTTY to collect information about those resources. You will also use Wireshark to capture packet data from the sessions you establish with PuTTY.

Learning Objectives

Upon completing this lab, you will be able to:

- Develop a plan for identifying and documenting the logical IP network design and IP addressing schema based on data collected from Lab #1
- Use PuTTY to establish Telnet and SSH to the IP addresses of the identified interfaces on Cisco routers, switches, and firewalls
- Use Cisco show commands to display the MAC-layer addresses of Ethernet ports, IP addressing schema, and subnet mask addressing used throughout the IP networking infrastructure
- Document the MAC addresses and IP addresses of the IP networking infrastructure
- Document the IP host addresses of the VM server farm hosts

TOOLS AND SOFTWARE USED

NAME	MORE INFORMATION
Wireshark	http://www.wireshark.org/
PuTTY	http://www.chiark.greenend.org.uk/~sgtatham/putty/
Cisco IOS	http://www.cisco.com/warp/cpropub/45/tutorial.htm

Deliverables

Upon completion of this lab, you are required to provide the following deliverables to your instructor:

1. A completed Network Documentation Chart #1;
2. Lab Assessment Questions & Answers for Lab #2.

Hands-On Steps

1. This lab begins at the student landing vWorkstation virtual machine desktop of the VSCL, as shown here.

FIGURE 2.1

"Student Landing" VSCL workstation

> **Note:**
> Review the Network Documentation Chart at the end of this lab. You will use the steps in this lab to find the information required to complete this deliverable.

2. To start the Wireshark application, **double-click** on the **Wireshark icon** on the desktop.
3. When the Wireshark window appears, **click** the **Citrix Systems link** in the area marked "Interface List." This tells Wireshark which interface to monitor for activity. In this case, you are capturing data from the virtual environment. In a production environment, you would see a list of interfaces corresponding to the resources available in that environment (servers, nodes, etc.).

FIGURE 2.2

The Wireshark window

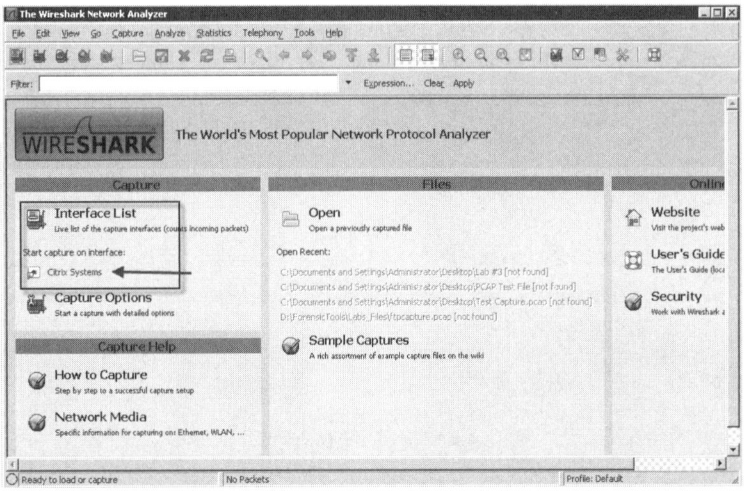

Once you select Citrix Systems, Wireshark begins capturing data, which you will see as lines of information in the application window.

4. **Minimize** the **Wireshark application window**.
5. Start the Windows Command Prompt by **clicking Start** > **Run** and **typing cmd** in the dialog box.

> **Note:**
> To collect data for analysis, Wireshark must have a stream of incoming packets to capture. The next steps cover how to feed IP packets to Wireshark using ping, Telnet, and Secure Shell (SSH) connections. These connections generate packets on the virtual environment interface, which are then captured by Wireshark.

6. From the Windows Command Prompt application window, **type ping 172.30.0.8** and **press Enter**. Note the Reply responses, which indicate the two-way passage of packets. You will use this information to complete the deliverables for this lab.

FIGURE 2.3

Windows Command Prompt window

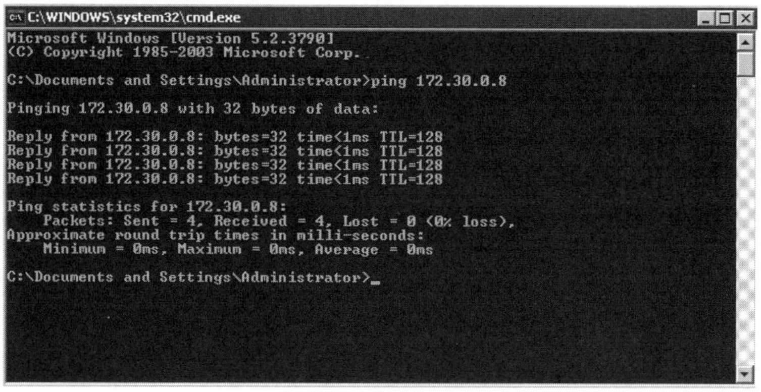

7. Next, **type ping 172.30.0.200** and **press Enter**. Note again the Reply responses. **Minimize** the **Windows Command Prompt window**. You will use this information to complete the deliverables for this lab.
8. You've now created a packet stream for Wireshark.
9. **Double-click** the **PuTTY icon** on the desktop to start the PuTTY application.

> **Note:**
> The next steps use PuTTY, a terminal emulator program that you can use as a client to create a variety of secure connections to network resources. This lab uses it to create Telnet and SSH sessions.

10. In the PuTTY application window, **type** the IP address for LAN Switch 1, **172.16.8.5**. **Select** the **Telnet radio button** and **click** the **Open button** to start the connection.

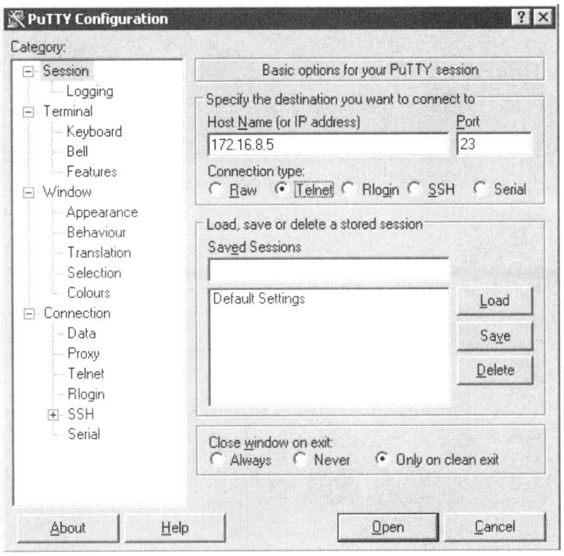

FIGURE 2.4
PuTTY application window

11. PuTTY will launch a terminal console window. At the login prompt, **type** the following:
   a. Username: **cisco**
   b. Password: **cisco**

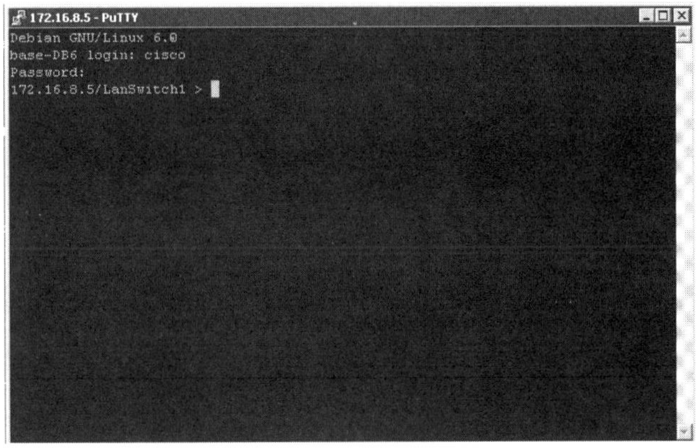

FIGURE 2.5
PuTTY terminal console window

Note:
The next steps involve using the Cisco IOS *show* command to obtain network documentation information from the interface you've connected to (LAN Switch 1). Cisco IOS is a package of routing, switching, and networking commands integrated with a Cisco-specific operating system, of which the *show* command is a key function. Entering a *show* command at the command prompt in the terminal console will return network information specific to the command you entered. There are hundreds of *show* commands in Cisco IOS; availability is based on the privilege level of the user. The relevant *show* commands for this lab include the following:

- *Show interface:* This command displays physical and logical configuration information about each interface and whether or not the interface is up or down. This commands tells you what interfaces are enabled and active;
- *Show IP interface:* This command displays logical IP address and subnet mask address information. It tells you what the IP subnet number, IP host address, and subnet mask address information is for all enabled ports;
- *Show IP ARP:* This command displays the address resolution table of MAC-layer addresses to assigned IP host addresses;
- *Show IP route:* This command displays the IP routing protocol used, the IP routes and network numbers visible to the switch/router, and the physical interface that an IP packet traverses based on the IP routes and IP networks seen (Cisco routers only);
- *Show VLAN:* This command displays the VLANs configured within the LAN Switch 1 and LAN Switch 2 devices only;
- *Show switch VLAN*: This command displays the VLANS configured within the ASA devices only.

12. In the terminal console window, at the command prompt labeled "172.16.8.5/LanSwitch1>," **type** the first Cisco IOS show command (**show interface**) found in the Command column of the following table and **press Enter**.

    Review the output for this command, being sure to look for the following information and **use** the data to complete the deliverables for this lab. **Repeat this step** for **each of the show commands** in this table:

COMMAND	DATA TO LOOK FOR AND REVIEW
show interface	Interface names, number of interfaces, interface up or down (available or unavailable)
show ip interface	Interface names, interface up or down, IP address, subnet mask address
show vlan	VLAN name, VLAN status
show ip arp	IP address, MAC-layer hardware address, interface name(s)

FIGURE 2.6

Data from Cisco IOS show commands

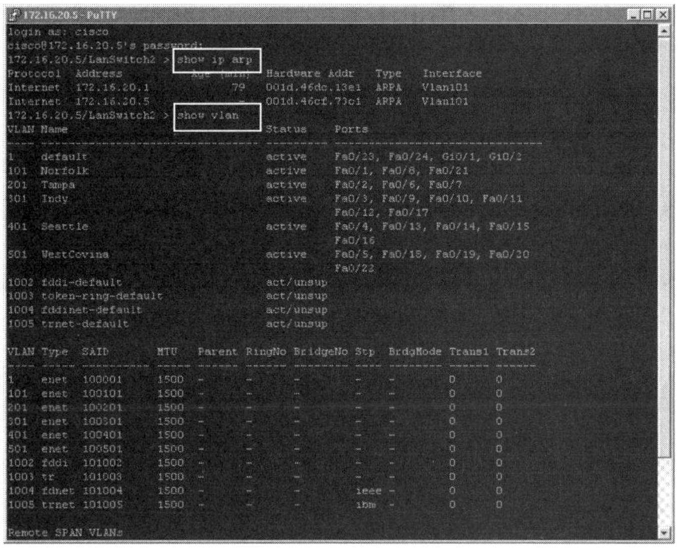

13. When finished entering the show commands and reviewing the output, **type quit** to close the terminal console.
14. **Double-click** the **PuTTY icon** to restart the application. This time, in the PuTTY application window, **type** the IP address for LAN Switch 2, **172.16.20.5**, **select** the **SSH radio button,** and **click** the **Open button** to start the connection. **Enter** the **username and password** from Step 11.
15. **Repeat** the **command entry process** from Step 12, reviewing the returned output for the same data to complete the deliverables for this lab. When finished, **type quit** to close the terminal console.
16. **Maximize** the **Wireshark application window** from the vWorkstation application tray.
17. **Click** the **Stop scan icon** to stop the packet capture process.

    Review the packet capture data in the Wireshark window, paying close attention to IP host address information, IP source and destination address information, and IP data payload information. You will need this information to complete the deliverables.

FIGURE 2.7

Packet capture data in the Wireshark window

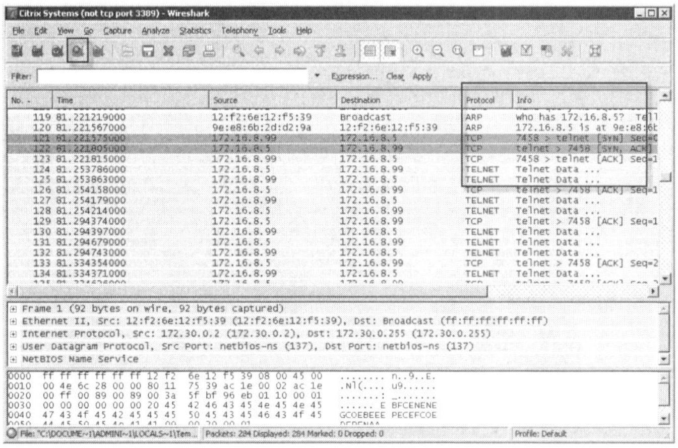

Note:

As you review the packet capture data from Wireshark, it will be helpful to consider the following things:

1. How can this information be used to compromise the Cisco LAN Switch 1 and LAN Switch 2 devices?
2. How can a protocol analyzer like Wireshark provide useful information to an attacker trying to break into the IP network infrastructure?

2

Network Documentation

Evaluation Criteria and Rubrics

The following are the evaluation criteria and rubrics for Lab #2 that students must perform:

1. Was the student able to develop a plan for identifying and documenting the logical IP network design and IP addressing schema based on data collected from Lab #1? – **[20%]**
2. Was the student able to use PuTTY to establish Telnet and SSH to the IP addresses of the identified interfaces on Cisco routers, switches, and firewalls? – **[20%]**
3. Was the student able to use Cisco show commands to display the MAC-layer addresses of Ethernet ports, IP addressing schema, and subnet mask addressing used throughout the IP networking infrastructure? – **[20%]**
4. Was the student able to document the MAC addresses and IP addresses of the IP networking infrastructure? – **[20%]**
5. Was the student able to document the IP host addresses of the VM server farm? – **[20%]**

LAB #2 – ASSESSMENT WORKSHEET

Network Documentation

Course Name and Number: ______________________

Student Name: ______________________

Instructor Name: ______________________

Lab Due Date: ______________________

Overview

One of the most important first steps in designing and implementing a layered security strategy is to perform a reconnaissance of the IP network infrastructure. This reconnaissance task is important to verify the physical and logical configuration of the networking infrastructure. This lab required the student to analyze and figure out—as if it were a puzzle—what the logical IP network design and configuration are. Students emulated what attackers do when performing an IP networking reconnaissance mission.

Lab Assessment Questions & Answers

1. What is the terminal console password for LAN Switch 1 and LAN Switch 2?

____

____

____

____

2. Specify the host IP address for LAN Switch 1 and LAN Switch 2 that you discovered from the Wireshark protocol capture file.

____

____

____

____

3. When you Telnet to LAN Switch 1 or LAN Switch 2, why is it a good idea to first ping an IP interface or port's IP address?

4. Why is using Telnet a security risk for an IP network infrastructure?

5. How can you mitigate the security risk caused by Telnet?

6. What is the difference between the following Cisco IOS commands: show interface and show IP interface?

7. What is your assessment (strong—good—weak) of the physical and logical network design from a CIA perspective? For integrity, limit the scope to the integrity of the Cisco software configurations.

8. Which Cisco IOS command displays the MAC-layer addresses that are resolved on that IP subnetwork?

9. How can you find out what the MAC-layer addresses and IP host addresses are of the server farm devices?

10. Which device supported encrypted terminal console connections and was verified in your Wireshark protocol capture and analysis: LAN Switch 1 or LAN Switch 2?

LAB #2 – ASSESSMENT SPREADSHEET

Network Documentation Chart #1

IP NETWORK NUMBER:			SUBNET MASK ADDRESS:	
HOST DEVICE	ACTIVE PORTS	IP HOST ADDRESSES	MAC ADDRESSES	SUBNET NUMBER
ASA_Student				
ASA_Instructor				
LAN Switch 1				
LAN Switch 2				
Norfolk				
Indy				
Tampa				
Seattle				
West Covina				

Network Discovery and Reconnaissance Probing Using Zenmap GUI (Nmap)

LAB 3

Introduction

In this lab, you will learn how to use the Zenmap Graphical User Interface (GUI) for the free Nmap Security Scanner application. This application is an open source tool that automates network exploration to perform several different types of security audit scans of large IP networks. It works with targeted IP hosts, IP subnetworks, or an entire IP network infrastructure. Nmap uses raw IP packets as a reconnaissance tool to perform the following network discovery tasks:

- Identify what hosts are available on the network
- Identify what services (application name and version) those hosts are offering
- Identify what operating systems (and OS versions) they are running
- Identify what type of packet filters/firewalls are in use

Information systems security practitioners find it useful for routine tasks, such as taking network inventory, managing service upgrade schedules, and monitoring host or service uptime.

Learning Objectives

Upon completing this lab, you will be able to:

- Use Zenmap GUI to perform a targeted IP subnetwork Intense Scan
- Perform an IP and network host discovery, a port and services scan, and an OS fingerprint scan on a targeted IP subnetwork
- Review and assess the results of the IP host discovery, the port and services scan, and the OS fingerprint scan on the targeted IP subnetwork
- Save the Intense Scan report and IP host discovery graphic for submission as lab deliverables
- Make recommendations for mitigating the identified risks, threats, and vulnerabilities

TOOLS AND SOFTWARE USED

NAME	TEXTBOOK REFERENCE	MORE INFORMATION
Zenmap GUI		http://nmap.org/zenmap/

Deliverables

Upon completion of this lab, you are required to provide the following deliverables to your instructor:

1. The Lab #3 Nmap Scan.xml file;
2. The Lab #3 Topology Fisheye Chart.pdf file;
3. Lab Assessment Questions & Answers for Lab #3.

Hands-On Steps

1. This lab begins at the student landing vWorkstation virtual machine desktop of the VSCL, as shown here.

FIGURE 3.1

"Student Landing" VSCL workstation

2. To start the Zenmap GUI application, **double-click** on the **Nmap-Zenmap GUI icon** on the desktop.

   The Zenmap GUI window opens with two drop-down menus labeled Target and Profile:

   - The Target field allows you to specify or select the networks or subnets you want to connect to
   - The Profile field indicates the types of scans you can perform

3. From the **Target drop-down menu, select 173.30.0.0/24**, which is the subnet address for this lab. From the **Profile drop-down menu, select Ping scan.**
4. **Click** the **Scan button**.

FIGURE 3.2

The Zenmap window

Review the output for this command, which returns basic information about host availability and the MAC address. You will need this data to complete the deliverables for this lab.

5. To gather more detailed data, **select 173.30.0.0/24** from the **Target drop-down menu. Select Intense Scan** from the **Profile drop-down menu** and **click** the **Scan button**.

> **Note:**
>
> The **Intense Scan** can take 3 to 5 minutes to complete all 36 test scripts. When the scan has finished, Zenmap will display the **Nmap done** command.

FIGURE 3.3

Intense Scan of 172.30.0.0/24 IP subnetwork

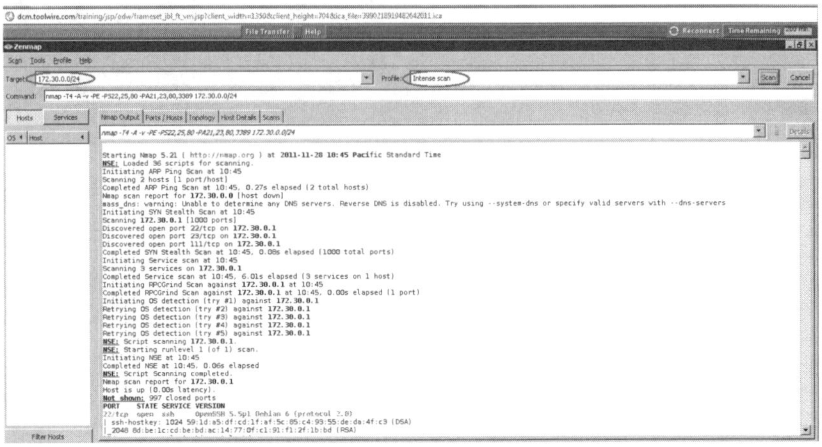

6. **Click Scan** on the main toolbar and **select Save Scan** to save the scan results. When the Save Scan dialog box opens, **name** the file **Lab #3 Nmap Scan** and **select Nmap XML files [*.xml]** from the drop-down menu. **Save** the file to the Security_Strategies folder **(My Computer > Local Disk (C:) > Security_Strategies)**.

FIGURE 3.4

Saving the Lab #3 Nmap Scan.xml file

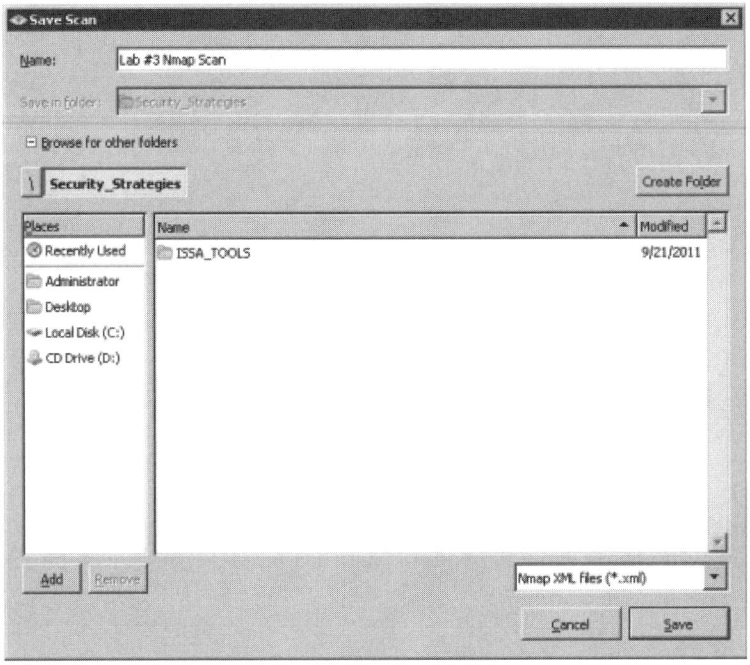

7. **Review** the output of the Intense Scan **by clicking** the **Ports/Hosts tab**. The data in this tab indicates whether ports are open and gives additional information about their state, service, and protocol. **Continue to review** the output, being sure to look for the following information in this **table**. You will use this data to complete the deliverables for this lab. **Repeat this step** for **each of the tabs** on this table.

TAB	DATA TO LOOK FOR AND REVIEW
Nmap Output	Raw Nmap outdata
Ports/Hosts	IP hosts and open ports
Topology	Fisheye bubble chart of IP hosts
Host Details	IP host OS fingerprint details
Scans	Completed scans performed

8. **Click** the **Topology tab**. This tab provides a fisheye bubble chart of all the IP hosts discovered during the scan. In this report, the bubble chart shows the relative size and connection type of all discovered hosts.

Note:
A **bubble chart** is a type of graph used to show relationships, by size, of different variables across an XY axis. A **fisheye** lens is a tool that can be used to change the shape and orientation of the graph.

9. **Click** the **Controls tab** and use the **Zoom** and **Ring Gap** slider controls in the lower right corner of the window to adjust the size and orientation of the chart.

Note:
As you will be saving a copy of this chart for a lab deliverable, your goal should be to produce a graphic in which all of the hostnames and the relationship indicators are readable, without any overlapping hostnames.

FIGURE 3.5
Topology fisheye bubble chart

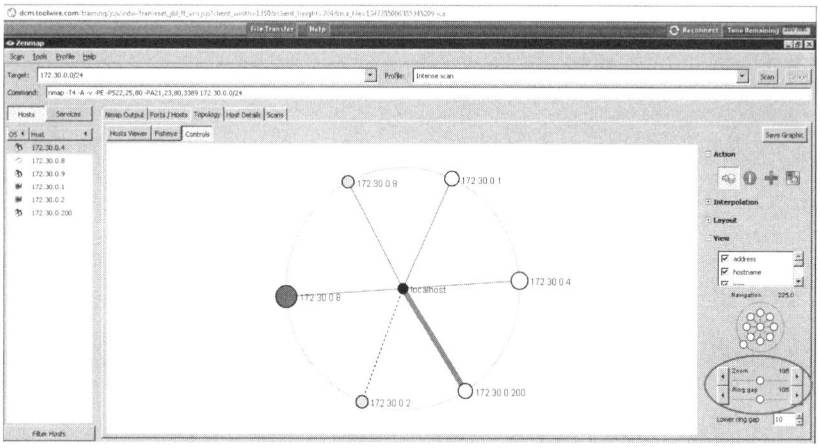

10. **Click** the **Save Graphic button**. You will need this file for the lab deliverables. When the Save Topology dialog box opens, **name** the file **Lab #3 Topology Fisheye Chart** and **select PDF** from the **Select File Type drop-down** menu. **Save** the file to the Security_Strategies folder **(My Computer > Local Disk (C:) > Security_Strategies)**.

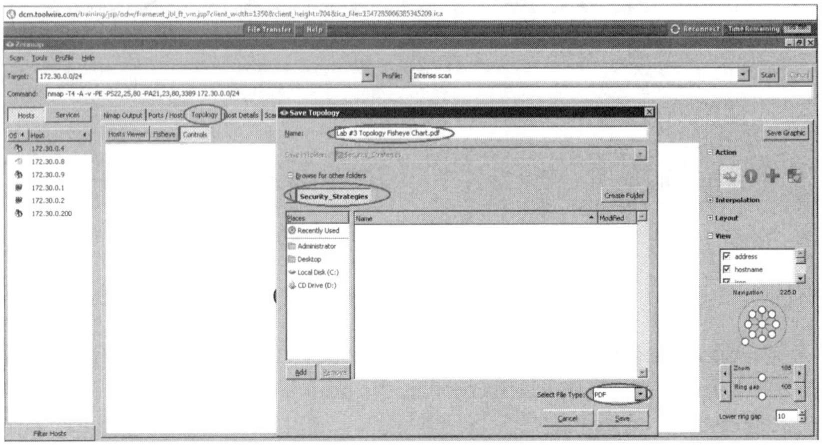

FIGURE 3.6

Save graphic of your topology fisheye bubble chart

11. **Close** the **Nmap application** and **download** the **Lab #3 Nmap Scan.xml** and **Lab #3 Topology Fisheye Chart.pdf** files using the **File Transfer** button and **submit** both as lab deliverables.

Evaluation Criteria and Rubrics

The following are the evaluation criteria and rubrics for Lab #3 that the students must perform:

1. Was the student able to use Zenmap GUI to perform a targeted IP subnetwork Intense Scan? – **[20%]**
2. Was the student able to perform an IP and network host discovery, a port and services scan, and an OS fingerprint scan on a targeted IP subnetwork? – **[20%]**
3. Was the student able to review and assess the results of the IP host discovery, the port and services scan, and the OS fingerprint scan on the targeted IP subnetwork? – **[20%]**
4. Was the student able to save the Intense Scan report and IP host discovery graphic for submission as lab deliverables? – **[20%]**
5. Was the student able to make recommendations for mitigating the identified risks, threats, and vulnerabilities? – **[20%]**

LAB #3 – ASSESSMENT WORKSHEET

Network Discovery and Reconnaissance Probing Using Zenmap GUI (Nmap)

Course Name and Number: ______________________________

Student Name: ______________________________

Instructor Name: ______________________________

Lab Due Date: ______________________________

Overview

One of the most important tools for information systems security practitioners is a packet capture application. This lab examined the strengths and weaknesses in an IP network design and implementation and how best to mitigate these weaknesses with best practices. After performing the initial IP network reconnaissance task, the second task was identifying the types of IP hosts, servers, operating systems, and applications. This lab demonstrated how information systems security practitioners perform network discovery and security scans. Students learned how to load and run Zenmap GUI (Nmap) security scanning software to perform an IP network security scan to identify risks, threats, and vulnerabilities within the IT infrastructure.

Lab Assessment Questions & Answers

1. What interfaces on LAN Switch 1 and LAN Switch 2 are configured with Telnet, and which interfaces are configured with SSH for remote terminal connectivity?

____

____

____

____

2. From your assessment in Lab #2 regarding the IP network design from a CIA perspective, what would you recommend to enhance CIA throughout the IP network infrastructure? For integrity, limit the scope to the Cisco device's software configuration.

____

____

____

____

____

3. Given the identified weaknesses from the IP network infrastructure and implementation of the Cisco devices, what recommendations would you make to mitigate the weaknesses?

4. What is the IP subnet number for the server farm VLAN where the classroom workstation with a virtualized server farm is located (ASA_Instructor VLAN)?

5. Explain both the information systems security practitioner and hacker perspectives of using a security scanning application such as Zenmap GUI (Nmap).

6. How many tests did your Intense Scan definition perform? List them all after reviewing the scan report.

7. Describe what each of these tests displays within the Zenmap GUI (Nmap) scan report.

8. How many total IP hosts (not counting Cisco device interfaces) did Zenmap GUI (Nmap) find on the network?

9. Did the Intense Scan match the total number of IP hosts on the server farm VLAN you found in Lab #2?

10. Fill in the network documentation chart on the following page for Lab #3 – Network Discovery and Reconnaissance Probing Using Zenmap GUI (Nmap):

LAB #3 – ASSESSMENT SPREADSHEET

Network Discovery and Reconnaissance Probing Using Zenmap GUI (Nmap) Chart #2

SERVER FARM HOST DEVICE	TYPE OF SERVER	OS AND VERSION	APPLICATIONS AND SERVICES ENABLED	PORTS AND STATUS

LAB 4

Perform a Software Vulnerability Scan and Assessment with Nessus®

Introduction

In this lab, you will learn how to perform vulnerability assessments using Nessus®, which is an application built specifically for network discovery of devices and the operating systems and software running on them. Nessus® performs remote scans and audits of Unix, Windows, and network infrastructures and can perform a network discovery of devices, operating systems, applications, databases, and services running on those devices.

Any noncompliant hosts running applications such as peer-to-peer, spyware, or malware (worms, Trojans, etc.) are detected and identified. Nessus® is capable of scanning all ports on every device and issuing remediation strategy suggestions as required. Nessus® includes the ability to perform in-depth Web application audits that identify vulnerabilities in custom-built applications.

Learning Objectives

Upon completing this lab, you will be able to:

- Launch and run the Nessus® vulnerability assessment scanner
- Configure a policy and scan definition using Nessus® as a vulnerability scanning and assessment tool to perform:
  - Network discovery
  - Port scanning
  - OS fingerprint scanning
  - Services scan
  - Software vulnerability scanning
- Generate a vulnerability assessment report of the targeted VM server farm as a lab deliverable
- Use the summary of findings generated by the Nessus® vulnerability scan to identify a solution to known vulnerabilities
- Document the VM server farm and its identified services, applications, open ports, and identified vulnerabilities in an HTML scan report

TOOLS AND SOFTWARE USED

NAME	MORE INFORMATION
Nessus®	http://www.Nessus.org/products/Nessus

Deliverables

Upon completion of this lab, you are required to provide the following deliverables to your instructor:

1. Homepage screenshot of the Nessus® vulnerability assessment scan (HTML format submitted in a text document);
2. Lab Assessment Questions & Answers for Lab #4.

Hands-On Steps

1. This lab begins at the student landing vWorkstation virtual machine desktop of the VSCL, as shown here.

FIGURE 4.1

"Student Landing" VSCL workstation

2. **Double-click** the **Nessus Server Manager icon** to launch the application.

FIGURE 4.2

The VSCL "Landing" vWorkstation: Connecting to Nessus®

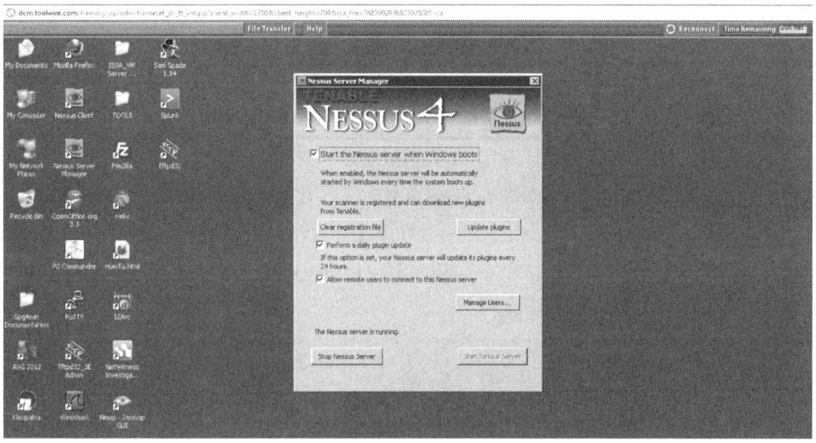

3. **Click** the **Manage Users button** on the Nessus Server Manager window to add a new user account.

4. In the Nesssus User Management dialog box, **click** on the **+ button** in the bottom left corner to open the **Add/Edit a user** dialog box.
5. **Type** the following login information:
   - User name: **administrator**
   - Password: **ISS316Security**
   - Password (again): **ISS316Security**
6. **Select** the **Administrator checkbox** to give this user administrative privileges.

FIGURE 4.3

Add/Edit a user in Nessus Server Manager

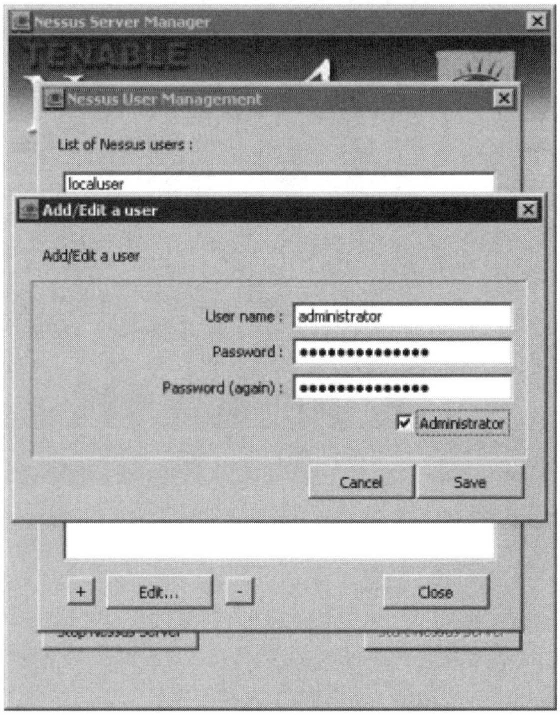

7. **Click** the **Save** button to finish creating the new user account, and then click **Close**.
8. **Close** the **Nessus Server Manager window**.
9. **Double-click** the **Mozilla Firefox icon** on the vWorkstation desktop to start the browser.
10. The Nessus Client is accessed using a secure Web browser connection. **Type** the following URL in the Firefox navigation bar to open the locally hosted Nessus® implementation, and then **press Enter**:
    - **https://localhost:8834**

Note:

The first time you connect to the Nessus Client, you will see a Web page that tells you that the connection you are about to make is untrusted. To proceed any further, you must add Nessus® to Firefox's exception list.

FIGURE 4.4

Untrusted connection dialog for Nessus®

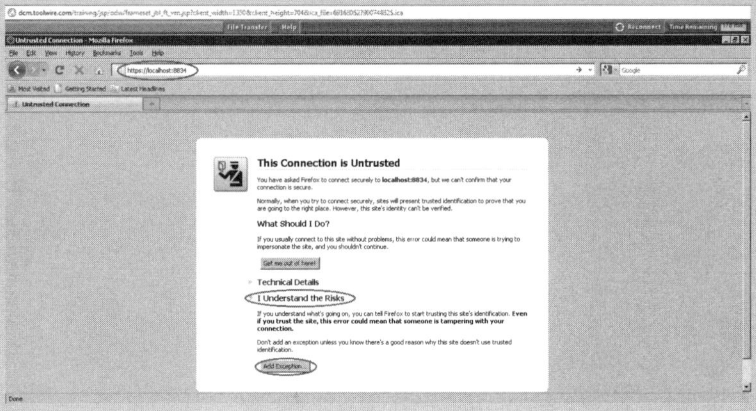

(Continues)

> Follow these steps to add the site to the exception list:
>
> 1. **Click I Understand the Risks** on the untrusted connection page to display the bottom half of the Untrusted connection window.
> 2. **Click** the **Add Exception button**.
> 3. In the **Add Security Exception** dialog box, make sure the **Permanently store this exception checkbox** is selected.
> 4. **Click** the **Confirm Security Exception** button to close the dialog box.
>
> The next time you use the Nessus Client, you will not have to complete these steps.

11. When the Nessus Client site appears, log in using the new user account you created in Steps 3–7:
    - User name: **administrator**
    - Password: **ISS316Security**

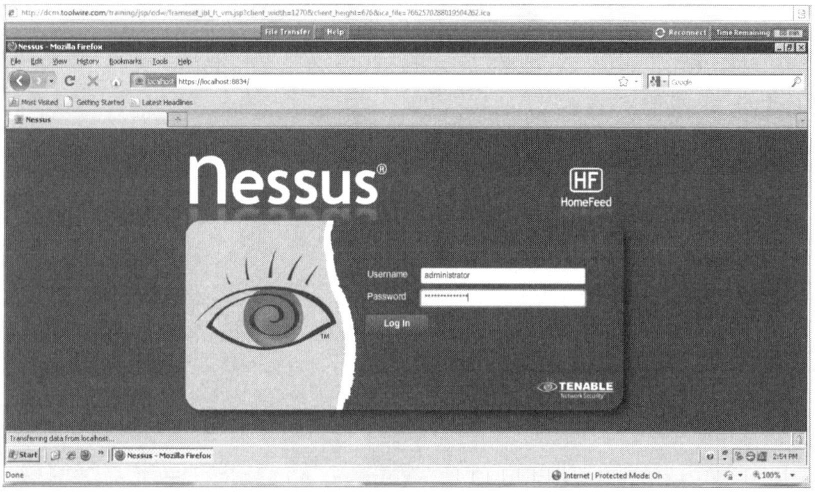

FIGURE 4.5

Log in to Nessus®

12. **Click** the **Log In button**.
13. **Click OK** to accept the Nessus HomeFeed Terms of Use and open the Nessus Client homepage.

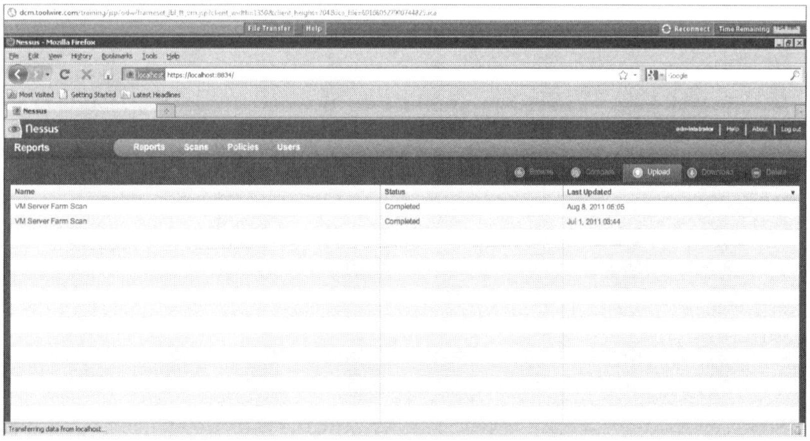

FIGURE 4.6

Nessus Client homepage

Note:
The next steps will create a custom security policy using the Nessus Client. This step, which configures the parameters for the scan, is required prior to conducting a vulnerability scan. These include:

- Parameters that control technical aspects of the scan such as timeouts, number of hosts, type of port scanner, and more
- Credentials for local scans (e.g., Windows, SSH), authenticated Oracle Database scans, HTTP, FTP, POP, IMAP, or Kerberos-based authentication
- Granular family or plug-in-based scan specifications
- Database compliance policy checks, report verbosity, service detection scan settings, Unix compliance checks, and more

14. **Click** the **Policies tab** on the Nessus Client homepage.
15. **Click** the **Add button** to add a new policy.
16. In the **Name** box, **type Lab #4 Nessus Policy**.

FIGURE 4.7
Creating Lab #4 Nessus Policy

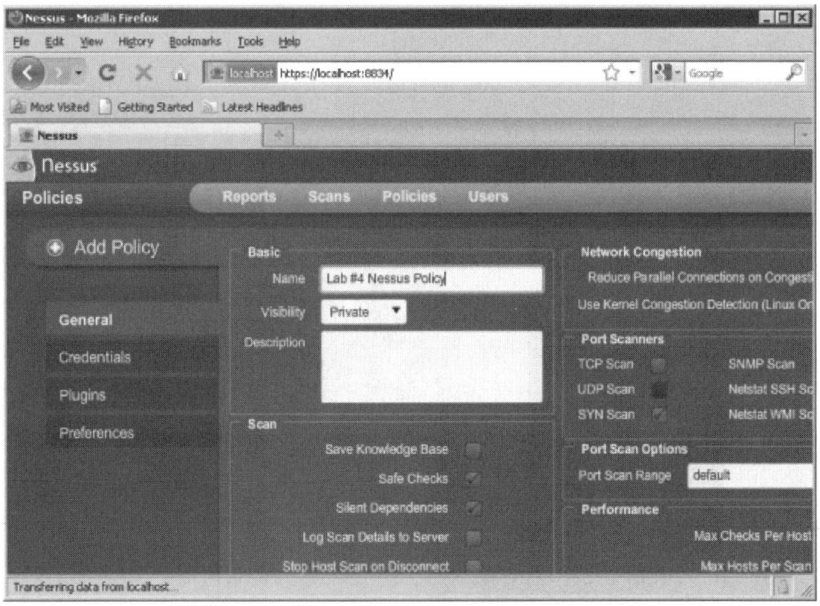

Note:
Note that there are four configuration tabs: General, Credentials, Plugins, and Preferences. For most environments, the default settings do not need to be modified, but selecting one of these tabs will provide options for more granular control over the Nessus® scanner operation as described in the following table.

TAB	CONFIGURABLE OPTIONS
General	Allows you to name your policy and define the scan-related operations.
Credentials	Allows you to configure the Nessus® scanner to use authentication credentials during scanning. Configuring credentials allows Nessus® to perform a wider variety of checks that result in more accurate scan results.
Plugins	Enables the user to choose specific security checks by plug-in family or individual checks.
Preferences	Displays further configuration items for the selected category. This is a dynamic list of configuration options that is dependent on the plug-in feed, audit policies, and additional functionality to which the connected Nessus® scanner has access.

17. **Click** the **Next button** to accept the default settings for the **General tab** and display the **Credentials tab**. **Explore** the configuration options, but do not make any adjustments or change any fields. **Repeat this step** for the **remaining tabs** described in the table.
18. **Save** the **Lab #4 Nessus Policy** parameters by **clicking Submit** on the final screen.

> **Note:**
> The next steps will set up a vulnerability scan and create a scan report.

19. **Click** the **Scans tab** on the Nessus Client homepage.
20. **Click** the **Add button** to add a new scan and configure the information described in the table.

FIELD LABEL	CONFIGURABLE OPTIONS
Name	Set the name that will be displayed in the Nessus UI to identify the scan.
Type	Choose between Run Now (immediately execute the scan after submitting) or Template (save as a template for repeat scanning).
Policy	Select a previously created policy that the scan will use to set parameters controlling Nessus® server scanning behavior.
Scan Targets	Targets can be entered by single IP address (192.168.0.1), IP range (192.168.0.1-192.168.0.255), subnet with CIDR notation (192.168.0.0/24), or resolvable host (www.Nessus.org).
Targets File	A text file with a list of hosts can be imported by clicking on Browse and selecting a file from the local machine. Example host file formats and individual hosts include: • 192.168.0.100, 192.168.0.101, 192.168.0.102 • Host range: 192.168.0.100-192.168.0.102 • Host CIDR block: 192.168.0.1/24

21. In the **Name** box, **type Lab #4 Nessus Scan**.
22. In the **Type** box, **select Run Now** from the drop-down menu.
23. In the **Policy** box, **select Lab #4 Nessus Policy** from the drop-down menu.
24. In the **Scan Targets** box, **type 172.30.0.0/24**.
25. Leave the **Targets File** box empty.

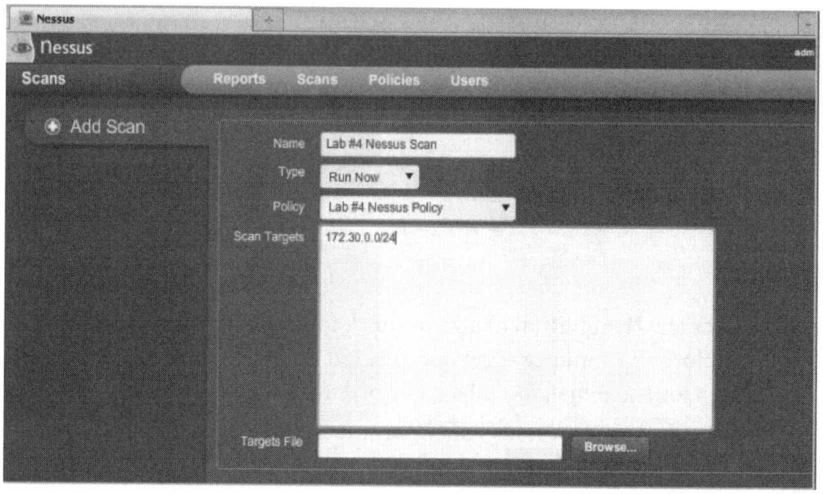

FIGURE 4.8

Creating parameters for Lab #4 Nessus Scan

26. **Click** the **Launch Scan button** to start the scan.

    The scan will begin immediately and a status bar, colored yellow, will indicate the progress of the scan.

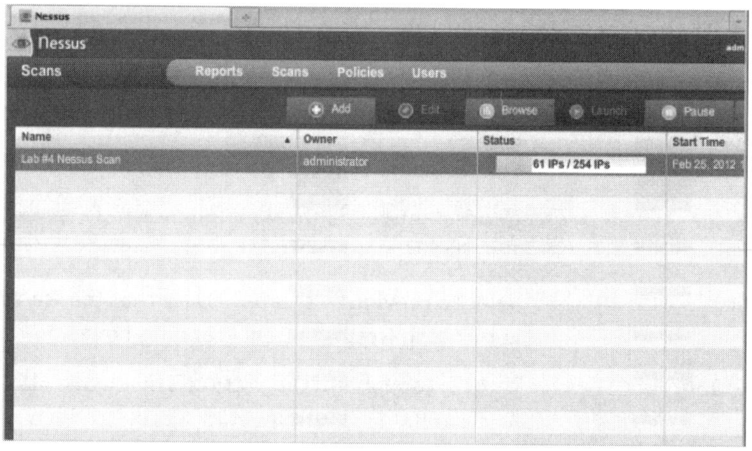

FIGURE 4.9

Nessus Scan progress bar

> **Note:**
> You can use the control buttons at the top of the Scans screen to Pause, Resume, or Stop the scan. Use the Browse button to see more detail about the progress of the scan for each target being scanned.

27. **Click** the **Reports tab** in the toolbar at the top to show the running and completed scans. The Reports screen acts as a central point for viewing, comparing, uploading, and downloading scan results.

28. **Double-click** the **Lab #4 Nessus Scan** line item to open the report for that scan.

    The first screen you see is the summary screen, which gives an overview of hosts scanned and vulnerabilities discovered. Vulnerabilities are categorized according to severity: High, Medium, and Low.

> **Note:**
> You can also access the scan report by first clicking on the report name and then clicking the Browse button.

FIGURE 4.10

Nessus® report summary

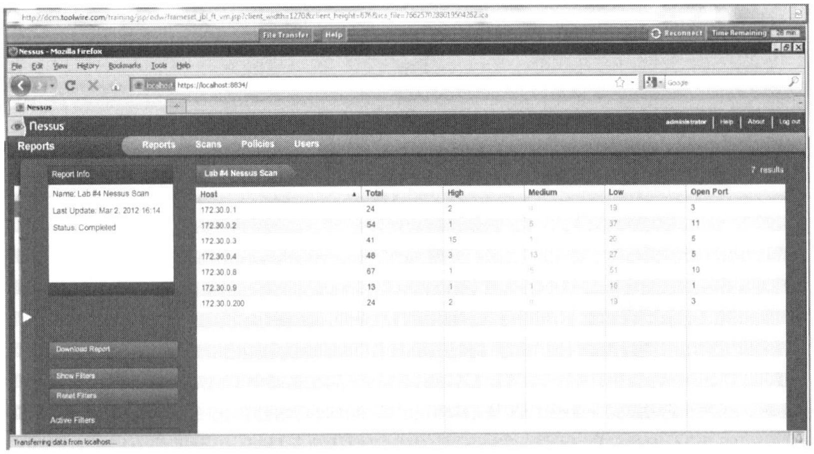

29. **Click** the **High column header** to sort the Hosts by vulnerability level. This will display the host with the greatest number of high-severity vulnerabilities at the top of the list.

> **Note:**
> Clicking a column header will toggle the displayed results either in descending order (greatest to least) or in ascending order (least to greatest). If you clicked the High column header in Step 29 and found your results displayed in ascending order, click the column header again to change the order and proceed to the next step.

30. **Double-click** the host at the top of the list to open the report's detail screen.

    Just below the Nessus® toolbar, on the Reports screen, you will see a "breadcrumb trail" of report pages. This trail is displayed as a series of clickable arrows.

FIGURE 4.11

"Breadcrumb trail" of Nessus® reports

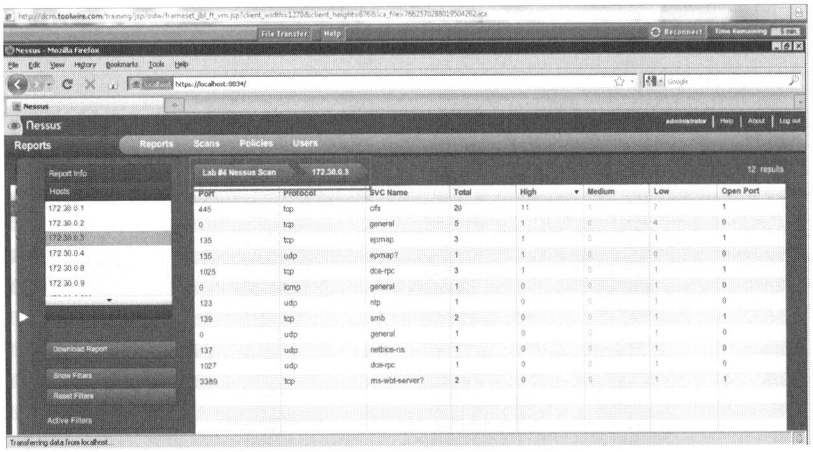

31. On the host detail screen, sort the port numbers by severity level by **clicking** the **High column header**.
32. **Click** the port number with the greatest number of high-severity vulnerabilities.

    The summary of findings displays the Nessus Plugin ID, vulnerability name, port, protocol, and severity for TCP port 445.
33. Sort the summary of findings by **clicking** on the **Severity** column header to list the high-severity vulnerabilities first.

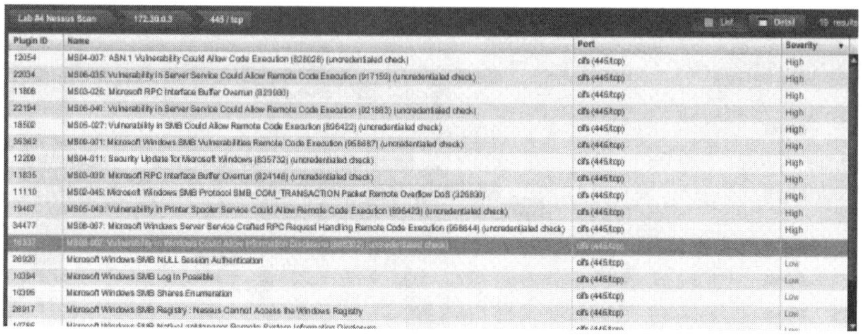

FIGURE 4.12

Summary of findings for host 172.30.0.3, port 445

34. **Click** on the first vulnerability at the top of the list.

    Selecting a vulnerability from the list will display full details of the finding, including a technical description, references, solution, detailed risk factor, and any relevant output. The details in the vulnerability Plugin ID provides overview, solution, risk factor, and CVE listing information.

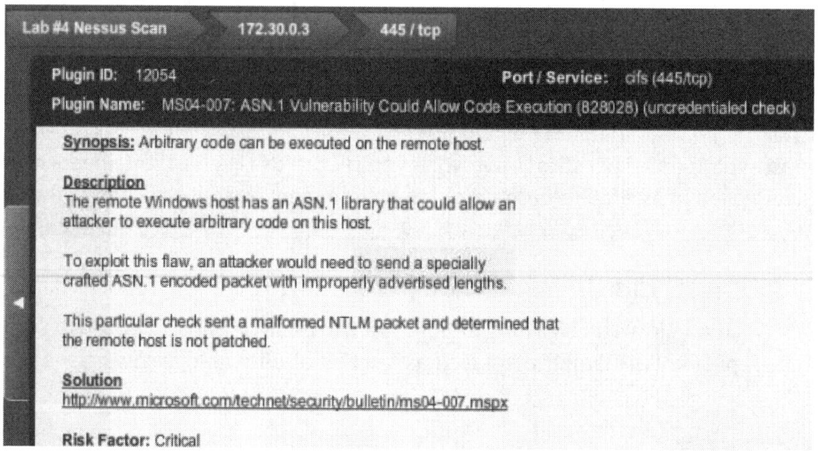

FIGURE 4.13

Full details for Plugin ID 12054

35. **Click** the **Lab #4 Nessus Scan arrow** in the breadcrumb trail at the top of the report to return to the report summary homepage.
36. **Click** the **Download Report button** on the left-hand menu to save a copy of the report. You will need this file for the deliverables of this lab.

37. In the Download Report dialog box, **select HTML export** from the drop-down menu and **click Submit**.

FIGURE 4.14

Download your Nessus® scan report

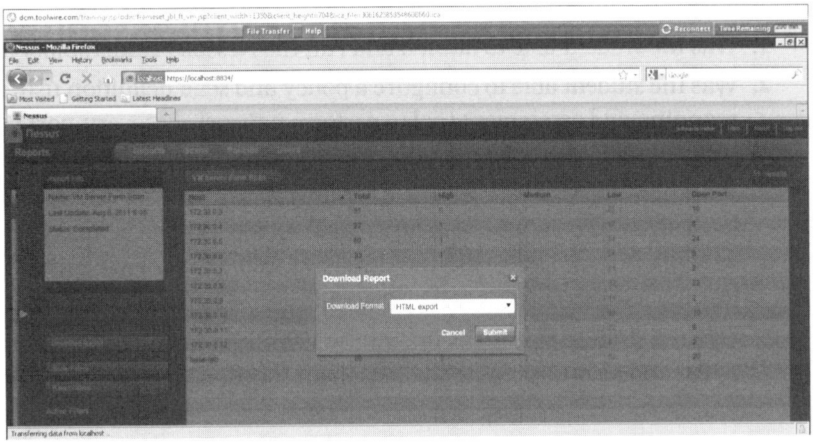

38. **Make a screen capture** of the front page of the **HTML report** and **paste** it into a text document. **Submit** it to your instructor as a deliverable. Make sure to show the listing of all IP hosts.

> **Note:**
> To capture the screen, **press** the **Ctrl** and **PrtSc** keys together, and then **use Ctrl + V** to paste the image into a Word or other word processor document.

FIGURE 4.15

Front page of HTML export report, including list of hosts

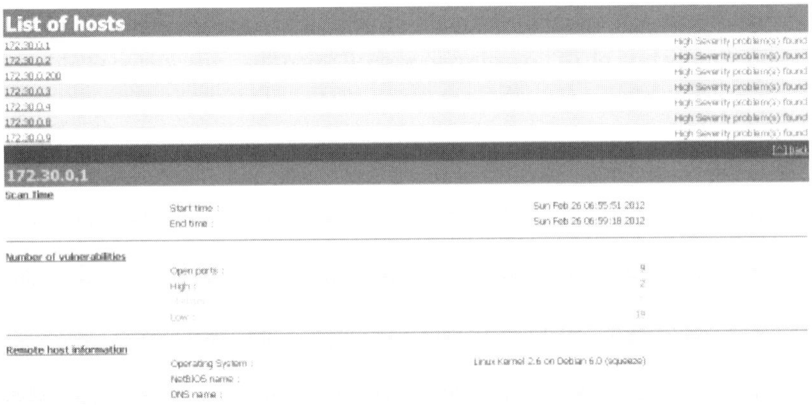

39. **Save** the document to the Security_Strategies folder (**My Computer > Local Disk (C:) > Security_Strategies**).
40. Use the **File Transfer button** on the vWorkstation desktop to transfer the document to your physical workstation.
41. **Close** the **Firefox browser window** to exit the Nessus Client.

3. What five things can you configure as part of a vulnerability scan?

4. Explain both the information systems security practitioner and hacker perspectives of using a security scanning application such as Nessus®.

5. How many tests does the Nessus® Lab #4 Nessus Scan perform?

6. Describe what each of these tests displays within the scan report details.

7. Briefly describe the process for identifying solutions to vulnerabilities uncovered by the Nessus® scan.

8. How many total IP hosts (not counting Cisco device interfaces) did you find on the server farm VLAN using the Nessus® Lab #4 Nessus Scan?

____

____

____

____

9. Fill in the following network documentation chart on the next page for Lab #4 – Perform a Software Vulnerability Scan and Assessment with Nessus®.

LAB #4 – ASSESSMENT SPREADSHEET

Perform a Software Vulnerability Scan and Assessment with Nessus®

SERVER FARM HOST DEVICE	TYPE OF SERVER	O/S & VERSION	IDENTIFIED VULNERABILITY	SUGGESTED REMEDIATION

Configure a Microsoft® Windows Workstation Internal IP Stateful Firewall

LAB 5

Introduction

In this lab, you will determine the properties and behavior of the default Windows Firewall settings for your workstation, enable Windows Firewall on the vWorkstation computer, set specific values for blocking or enabling certain transactions, and test to ensure that Windows Firewall is working properly.

Learning Objectives

Upon completing this lab, you will be able to:

- Identify the features and functions of the Microsoft® Windows workstation internal IP stateful firewall
- Review the default settings for the Microsoft® Windows workstation internal IP stateful firewall
- Configure the internal firewall for the landing vWorkstation based on a policy definition
- Test and verify that the internal firewall settings are implemented correctly on the landing vWorkstation
- Assess whether a network IP stateful firewall and/or Microsoft® Windows workstation internal firewall can be implemented as part of a layered security strategy

TOOLS AND SOFTWARE USED

NAME	MORE INFORMATION
Microsoft® Windows Firewall	http://technet.microsoft.com/en-us/library/bb490861.aspx

Deliverables

Upon completion of this lab, you are required to provide the following deliverables to your instructor:

1. Windows Firewall default configuration spreadsheets;
2. A text document that includes the following:
    a. Screen capture of the Windows Firewall General tab;
    b. Screen capture of the Windows Firewall Exceptions tab;
    c. Screen capture of the Windows Firewall Advanced tab;
2. Lab Assessment Questions & Answers for Lab #5.

Hands-On Steps

1. This lab begins at the student landing vWorkstation virtual machine desktop of the VSCL, as shown here.

FIGURE 5.1

"Student Landing" VSCL workstation

2. To open the TargetWindows01 virtual machine, **double-click** the **ISSA_VM Server Farm_RDP icon** on the desktop.
3. **Double-click** the **TargetWindows01.rdp file**.

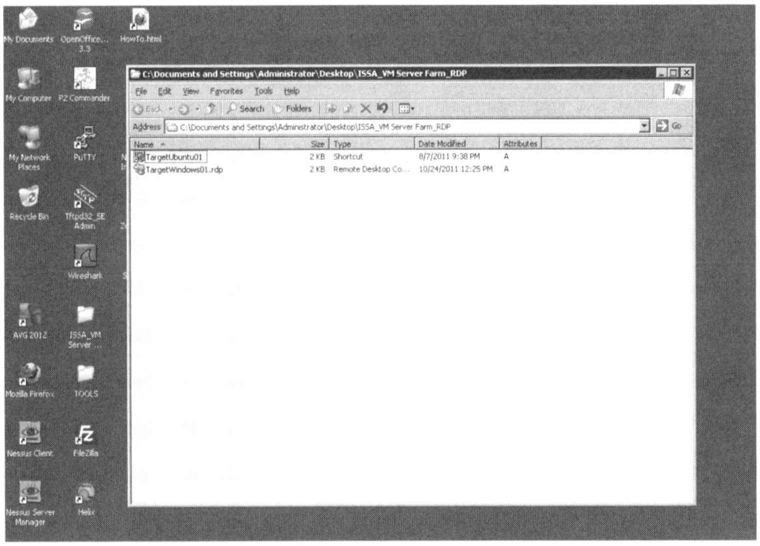

FIGURE 5.2

Open a remote desktop connection to the TargetWindows01 VM

4. **Log on** to the **TargetWindows01 VM** server with the following credentials and **press Enter**:
   - User name: **Administrator**
   - Password: **ISS316Security**

5. **Click OK** in the Connect to Server dialog box to start the FileZilla Server application.

FIGURE 5.3

Connect to Server dialog box

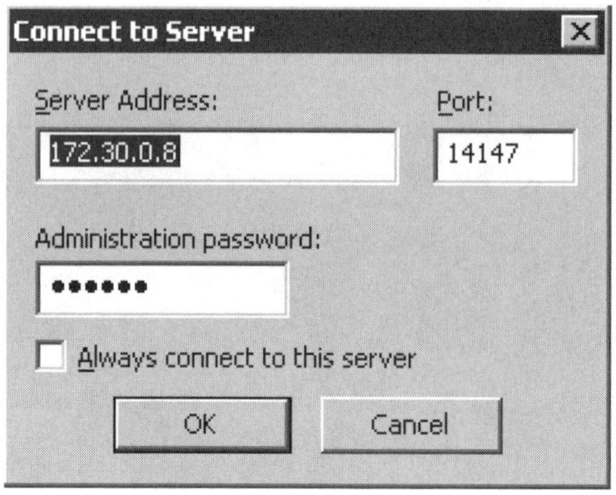

> **Note:**
> This dialog box loads automatically when the Windows server starts, with the address and password already filled in.

6. **Minimize** the **TargetWindows01 window**.

   The FileZilla Server application will continue to run in the background. You will need it later in this lab.

> **Note:**
> The next steps determine how the default Windows Firewall settings are configured on the vWorkstation and the Windows server. You will ping the Windows server from the vWorkstation, and then ping the vWorkstation from the Windows server.

7. **Close** the **ISSA_VM Server Farm_RDP window**.
8. From the vWorkstation desktop, **click** the **Windows Start button**.
9. **Select Run** from the menu.
10. **Type cmd** in the dialog box and **click OK**.

11. In the Windows Command Prompt window, ping the IP address for the TargetWindows01 server. **Type ping 172.30.0.8** and **press Enter**.

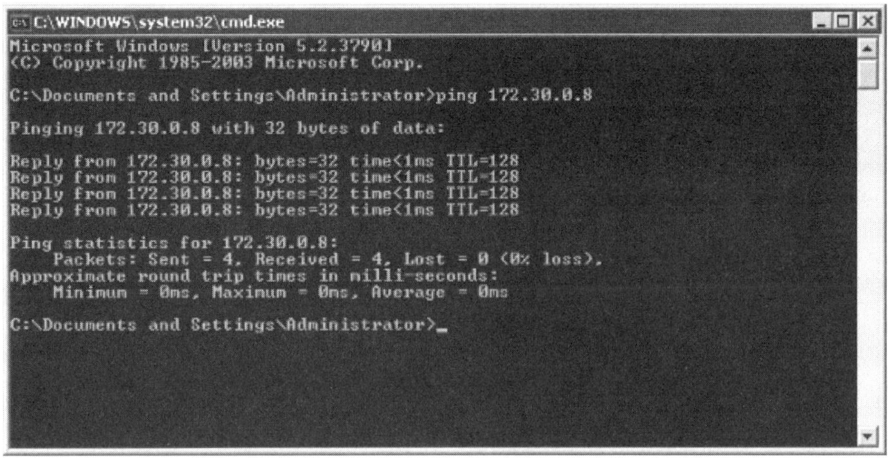

FIGURE 5.4

Successful ping of TargetWindows01

The replies indicate that the Windows server is accepting connections. It does not have Windows Firewall enabled.

12. **Close** the **Windows Command Prompt window**.
13. **Maximize** the **TargetWindows01 window**.
14. From the Windows server desktop, **click** the **Windows Start button**.
15. **Select Run** from the menu.
16. **Type cmd** in the dialog box and **click OK**.
17. In the Windows Command Prompt window, ping the IP address for the vWorkstation.
    Type ping 172.30.0.2 and **press Enter.**

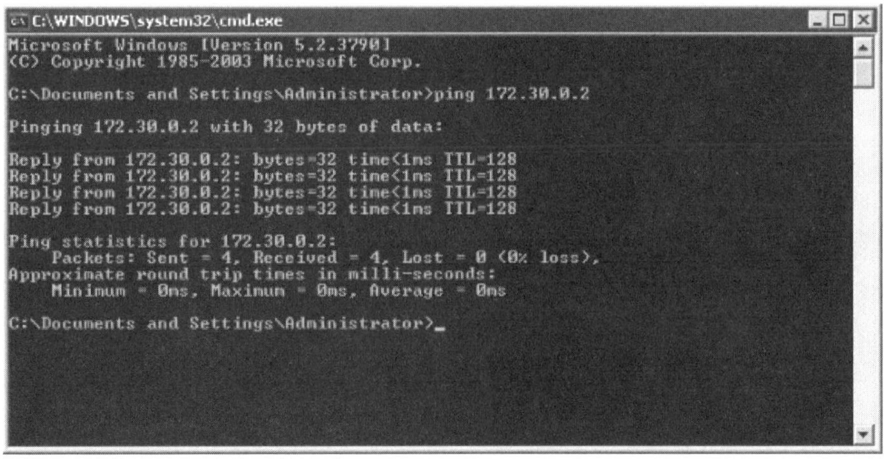

FIGURE 5.5

Successful ping of vWorkstation

The replies indicate that the vWorkstation is accepting connections and does not have Windows Firewall enabled.

18. **Close** the **Windows Command Prompt window**.

> **Note:**
> The next steps determine whether each computer is accepting file transfers, a more complex connection.

19. **Minimize** the **TargetWindows01 window** to switch back to the landing vWorkstation.
20. **Double-click** on the **FileZilla icon** on the desktop.
21. **Type** the following logon credentials in the address boxes at the top of the application window that opens to connect to the FileZilla Server on the TargetWindows01 server:
    - Host: **172.30.0.8**
    - User name: **student**
    - Password: **ISS316Security**
    - Port: **21**
22. **Click** the **Quickconnect button** to connect to the FileZilla Server.

FIGURE 5.6
Connecting to FileZilla Server on TargetWindows01 using FileZilla Client

23. **Double-click** the **Security_Strategies folder** in the Local site directory.
24. **Double-click** the **ISSA_TOOLS folder**.
25. **Double-click** the **Documentation folder**.
26. **Select** the **AnyConnect_adminguide.pdf file**.

27. **Drag** the **AnyConnect_adminguide.pdf file** and **drop** it into the **root directory folder** in the Remote site pane.

    The status responses in the area below the connection information indicate whether or not the file transfer was successful.

FIGURE 5.7

Successful FTP from vWorkstation to TargetWindows01

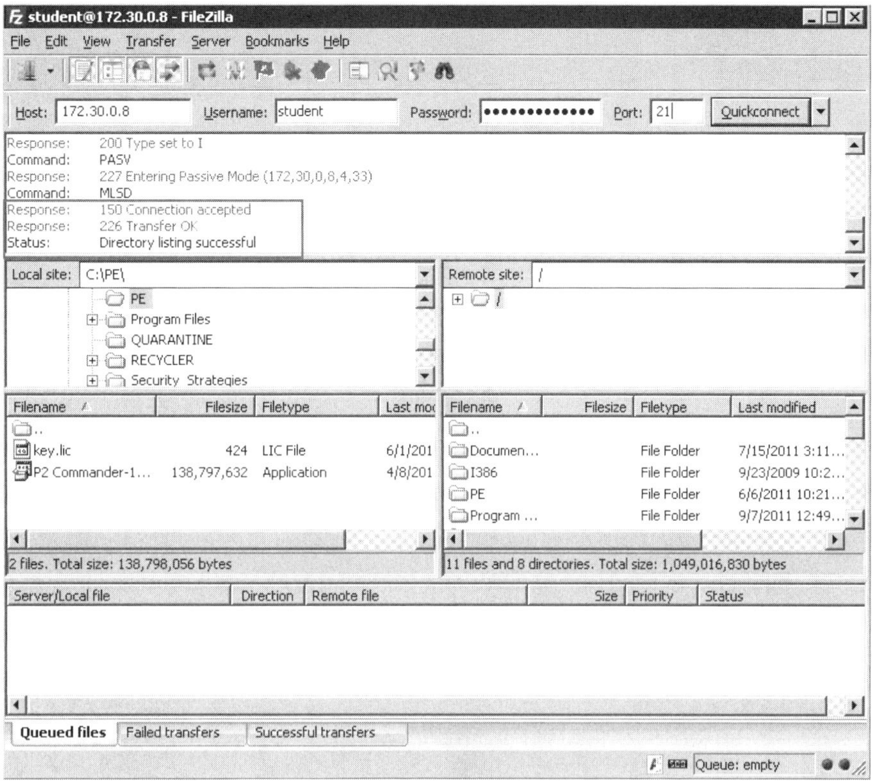

28. **Close** the **FileZilla Client window**.
29. **Maximize** the **TargetWindows01 window** to switch back to the TargetWindows01 desktop.
30. **Double-click** on the **My Computer icon**.
31. **Double-click Local Disk C:** and verify that the AnyConnect_adminguide.pdf you transferred appears in the directory.

> **Note:**
> The next steps demonstrate sending a file to the vWorkstation from TargetWindows01 using the Tftpd32 application.

32. **Double-click** the **Tftpd32_SE Admin icon** on the TargetWindows01 desktop to launch the application.

33. **Click** the **Tftp Client tab** to set up TargetWindows01 as the Tftp client.

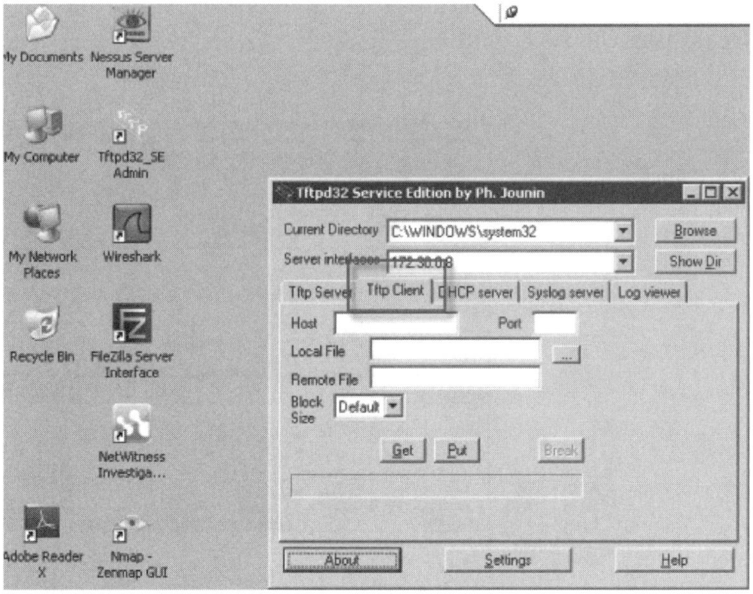

FIGURE 5.8

TargetWindows01 set as Tftp client

34. **Minimize** the **TargetWindows01 window** to switch to the vWorkstation desktop.
35. **Double-click** the **Tftpd32_SE Admin icon** on the vWorkstation desktop to launch the application.
36. **Click** the **Tftp Server tab**, if it's not already the active tab, to set up the vWorkstation as the Tftp server.

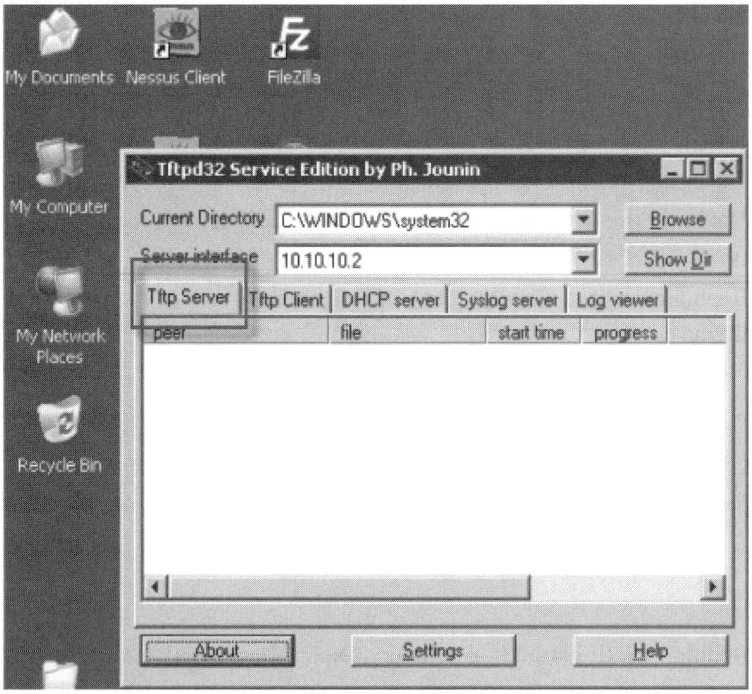

FIGURE 5.9

vWorkstation set as Tftp server

37. **Maximize** the **TargetWindows01 window** to switch back to the TargetWindows01 desktop.

38. **Type** the following logon credentials in the address boxes at the top of the application window that opens to connect to the vWorkstation Tftp Server in the Tftp Client tab:
    - Host: **172.30.0.2**
    - Port: **69**
    - Local file: **C:\AnyConnect_adminguide.pdf**

Note:
You can **click** the **File Select button** to the right of the Local File box to browse your computer for this correct file.

39. **Click** the **Put button** to start the Tftp transfer. A status response will pop up indicating a successful file transfer.

FIGURE 5.10
TFTP a file using Put

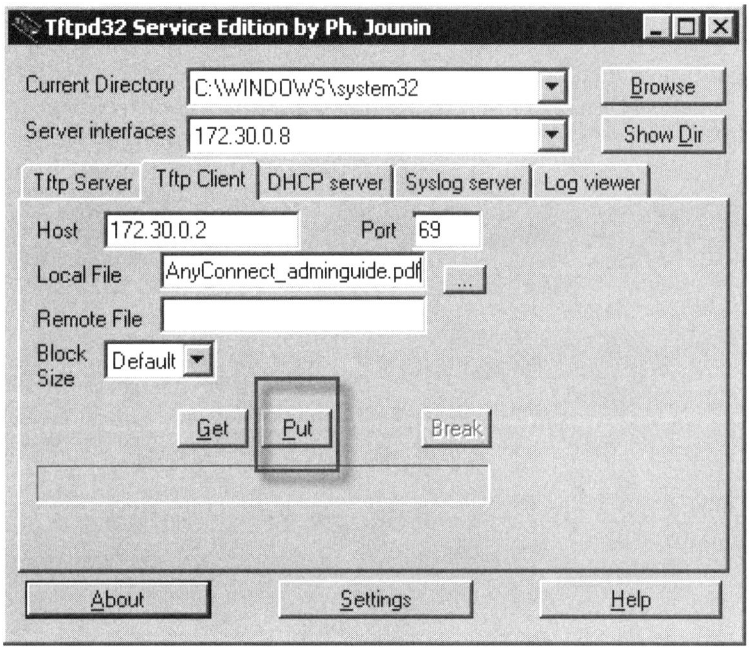

40. **Close** the **Tftpd32 window**.

Note:
The next steps demonstrate how to enable Windows Firewall on the vWorkstation and how to adjust the settings to limit or enable specific services.

41. **Minimize** the **TargetWindows01 window** to switch to the vWorkstation desktop.
42. **Click** the **Windows Start button.**
43. **Select Settings** from the menu.
44. **Click** on **Control Panel**.

45. **Scroll** to the bottom of the Control Panel window and **double-click** the **Windows Firewall icon**. Notice that the default setting for Windows Firewall is Off.

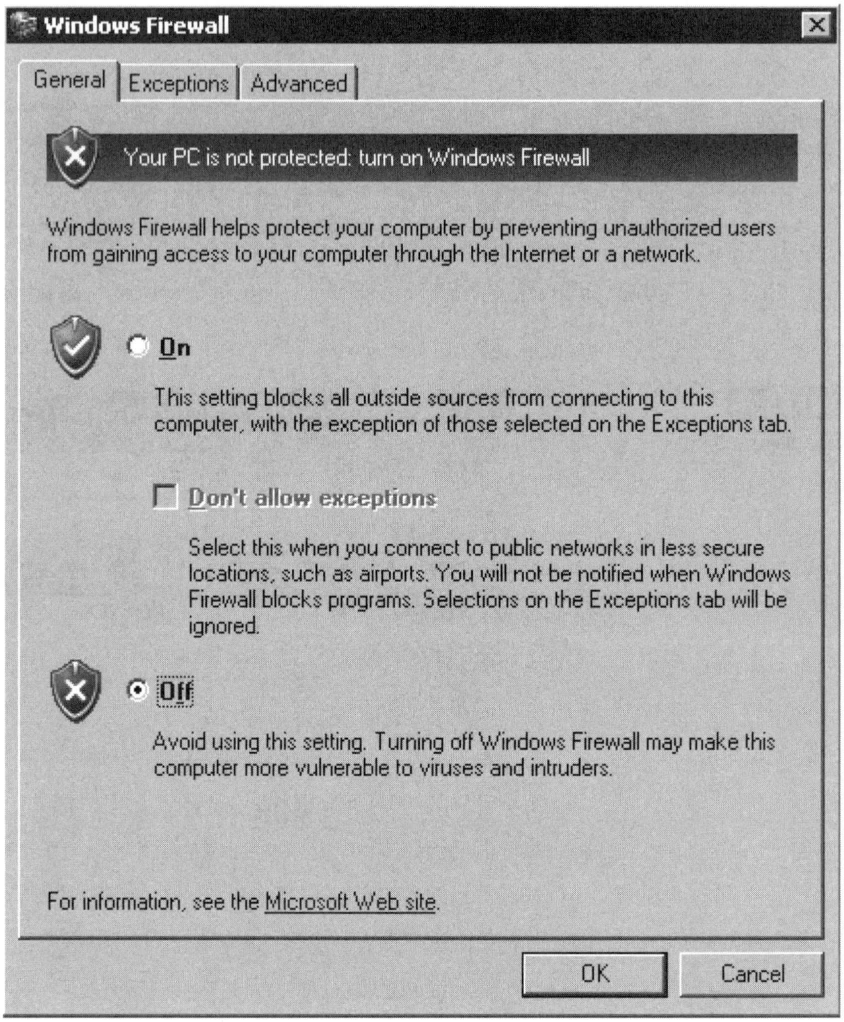

FIGURE 5.11 Default Windows Firewall General tab settings

46. **Make a screen capture** of the **Windows Firewall General tab** and **paste** it into a text document.

> **Note:**
> To capture the screen, **press** the **Ctrl** and **PrtSc** keys together, and then **use Ctrl + V** to paste the image into a Word or other word processor document.

47. **Select** the **On radio button** to enable Windows Firewall.
48. **Click** the **Exceptions tab** and **make a screen capture** of the settings on that tab and **paste** it into your text document.
49. **Click** the **Advanced tab** and **make a screen capture** of the settings on that tab and **paste** it into your text document.
50. **Save** the document to the Security_Strategies folder (**My Computer > Local Disk (C:) > Security_Strategies**).

51. Use the **File Transfer button** on the vWorkstation desktop to transfer the document to your physical workstation and submit it as a deliverable for this lab.

Note:
The next steps demonstrate how to enable FTP services while disabling ping, Telnet, and TFTP.

52. On the Advanced tab, **click** the **Settings button**.
53. On the Services tab, **click** the checkbox labeled **FTP Server**.

FIGURE 5.12
Enabling FTP Server in Windows Firewall

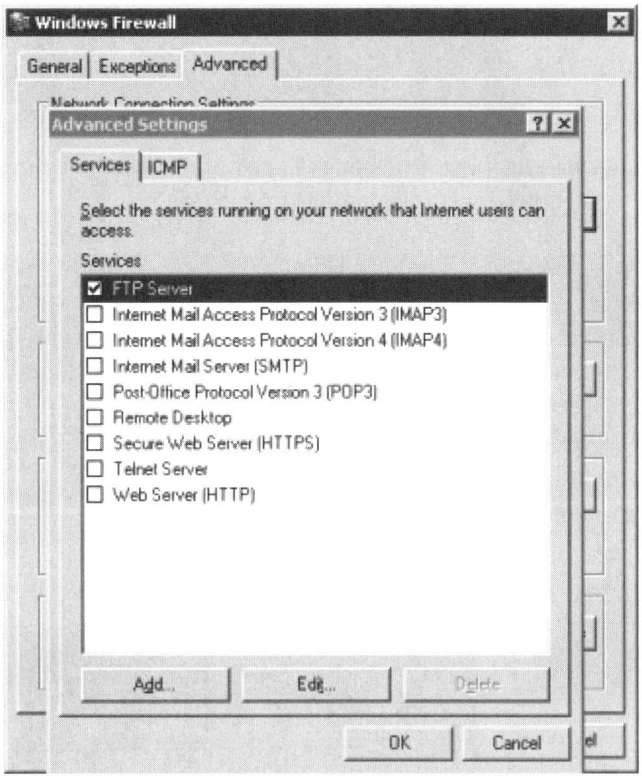

54. **Click OK** to confirm the new settings.
55. **Click OK** to close the **Windows Firewall window**.

Note:
The next steps demonstrate how to test the Windows Firewall settings on the vWorkstation and the Windows server using ping, FTP, and Tftp.

56. From the vWorkstation desktop, **click** the **Windows Start button**.
57. **Select Run** from the menu.
58. **Type cmd** in the dialog box and **click OK.**

59. In the Windows Command Prompt window, ping the IP address for the TargetWindows01 server. **Type ping 172.30.0.8** and **press Enter**.

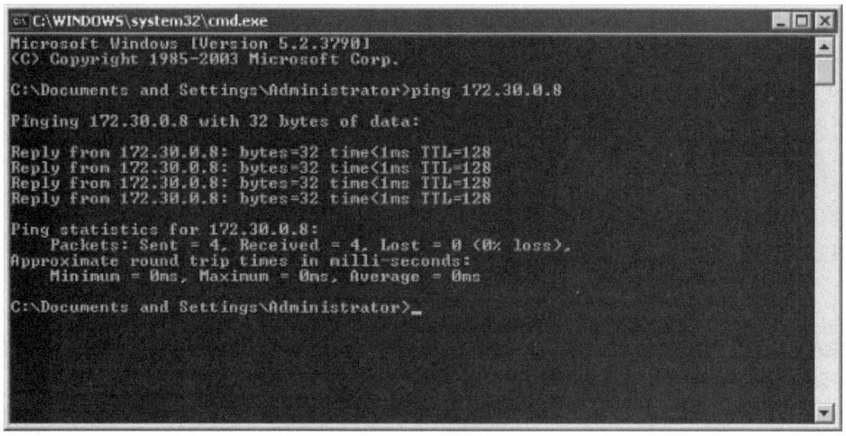

FIGURE 5.13

Ping attempt to TargetWindows01 showing successful replies

The replies indicate that it is still possible to ping outside resources from the vWorkstation (and that Windows Firewall is disabled on TargetWindows01).

Note:
The next steps repeat the same process, this time using the TargetWindows01 to ping the vWorkstation.

60. **Maximize** the **TargetWindows01 window** to switch back to the TargetWindows01 desktop.
61. **Select Run** from the menu.
62. **Type cmd** in the dialog box and **click OK**.
63. In the Windows Command Prompt window, ping the IP address for the vWorkstation. **Type ping 172.30.0.2** and **press Enter**

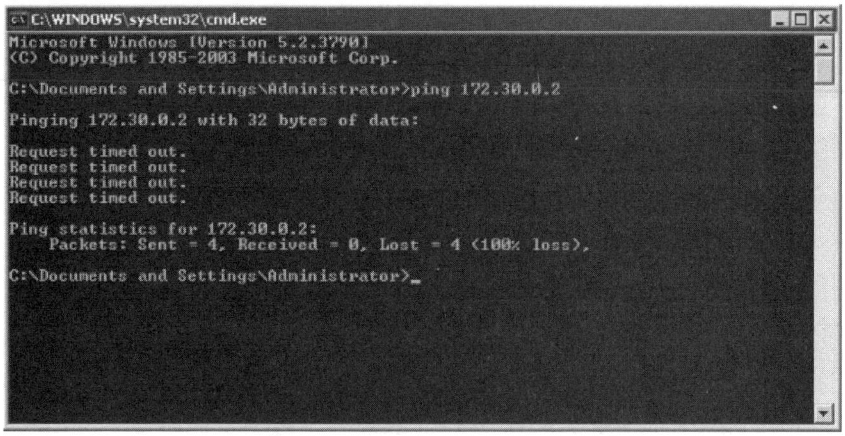

FIGURE 5.14

Ping attempt to vWorkstation showing request timeouts

The replies indicate that the requests have timed out. This indicates that ping is disabled by Windows Firewall on the vWorkstation.

64. **Close** the **Command Prompt window**.

Note:
The next steps will send a file via Tftp from the vWorkstation to TargetWindows01 using the Tftpd32 application.

65. **Double-click** the **Tftpd32_SE Admin icon**.
66. **Click** the **Tftp Client tab** to set up the Windows server as the Tftp client.
67. **Minimize** the **TargetWindows01 window** to switch to the vWorkstation desktop.
68. **Double-click** the **Tftpd32_SE Admin icon** on the vWorkstation desktop.
69. **Click** the **Tftp Server tab**, if it's not already the active tab, to set up vWorkstation as the Tftp server.
70. **Maximize** the **TargetWindows01 window** to switch back to the TargetWindows01 desktop.
71. **Type** the following information under the Tftp Client tab:
    - Host: **172.30.0.2**
    - Port: **69**
    - Local file: **C:\AnyConnect_adminguide.pdf**
72. **Click** the **Put button** to start the TFTP file transfer.

    The status response (block #0) indicates that the transfer was not successful, as Tftp is disabled via Windows Firewall on the vWorkstation.

FIGURE 5.15

Unsuccessful Tftp attempt to vWorkstation

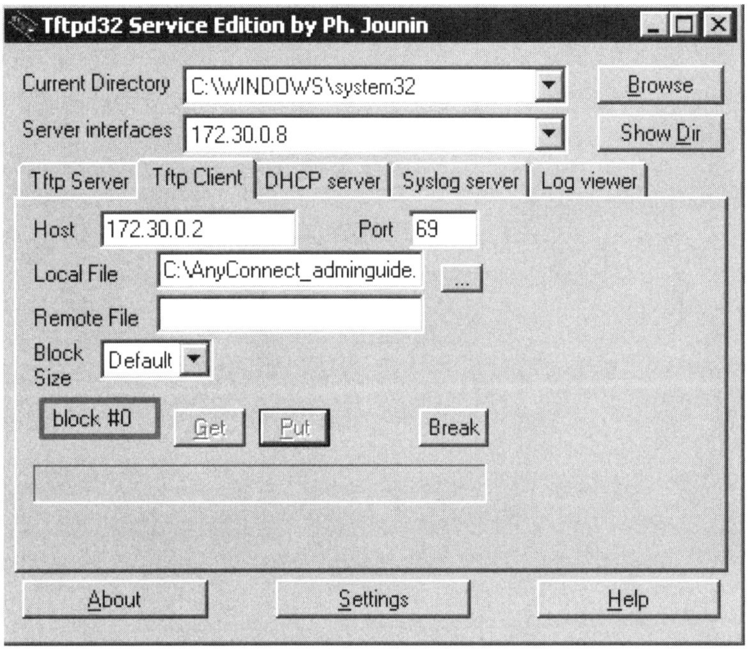

Note:
The next steps will transfer a file from the vWorkstation to TargetWindows01 using the FileZilla application.

73. **Minimize** the **TargetWindows01 window** to switch to the vWorkstation desktop.
74. **Double-click** the **FileZilla icon**.
75. **Type** the following information to log on to TargetWindows01:
    - Host: **172.30.0.8**
    - Username: **student**
    - Password: **ISS316Security**
    - Port: **21**
76. **Click** the **Quickconnect button**.
77. **Double-click** the **Security_Strategies folder** in the Local site directory.
78. **Double-click** the **ISSA_TOOLS folder**.

79. **Double-click** the **Documentation folder**.
80. **Select** the **AnyConnect_adminguide.pdf file**.
81. **Drag** the **AnyConnect_adminguide.pdf file** and **drop** it into the **root directory folder** in the Remote site pane.

    The status response in the top window indicates that the file transfer was successful. This indicates that FTP is enabled in the vWorkstation Windows Firewall.

FIGURE 5.16

Successful FTP from vWorkstation to TargetWindows01

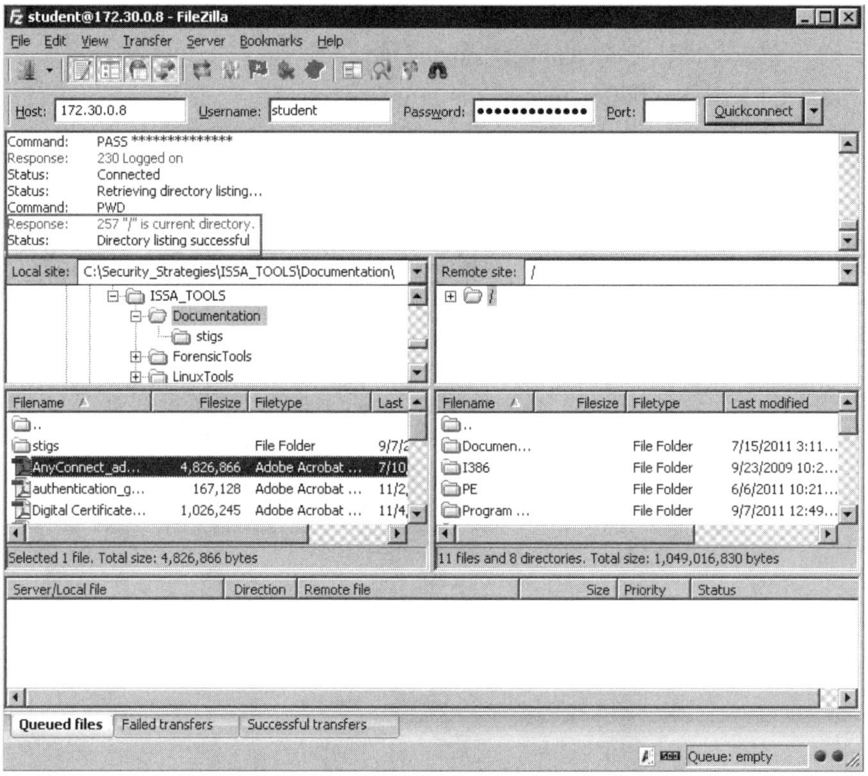

82. **Close** the **FileZilla application**.

Evaluation Criteria and Rubrics

The following are the evaluation criteria and rubrics for Lab #5 that the students must perform:

1. Was the student able to identify the features and functions of the Microsoft® Windows workstation internal IP stateful firewall? – [**20%**]
2. Was the student able to review the default settings for the Microsoft® Windows workstation internal IP stateful firewall? – [**20%**]
3. Was the student able to configure the internal firewall for the landing vWorkstation based on a policy definition? – [**20%**]
4. Was the student able to test and verify that the internal firewall settings are implemented correctly on the landing vWorkstation? – [**20%**]
5. Was the student able to assess whether a network IP stateful firewall and/or Microsoft® Windows workstation internal firewall can be implemented as part of a layered security strategy? – [**20%**]

LAB #5 – ASSESSMENT SPREADSHEET A

Configure a Microsoft® Windows Workstation Internal IP Stateful Firewall

Course Name and Number: ______________________________

Student Name: ______________________________

Instructor Name: ______________________________

Lab Due Date: ______________________________

Overview

Review the default settings for Windows Firewall on your student workstation and indicate your settings below:

GENERAL

_____ Recommended (Firewall On/Off)
_____ Don't Allow Exception Rules (On/Off)
_____ Not Recommended (On/Off)

EXCEPTIONS

_____ File Print Sharing
_____ Remote Assistance
_____ Remote Desktop
_____ uPnP Framework

ADVANCED

_____ Network Connection Settings:
    _____ 1394 Connections
    _____ Cisco AnyConnect VPN
    _____ Local Area Connection
    _____ Wireless Network Connection
_____ Security Logging:
    _____ Logging Options
    _____ Logging File Options
_____ ICMP:
    _____ Allow incoming request
    _____ Allow incoming time request
    _____ Allow incoming router request
    _____ Allow outgoing destination unreachable
    _____ Allow outgoing source quench
    _____ Allow outgoing parameter problem
    _____ Allow outgoing time exceeded
    _____ Allow redirect
    _____ Allow outgoing packet too big

LAB #5 – ASSESSMENT SPREADSHEET B

Configure a Microsoft® Windows Workstation Internal IP Stateful Firewall

Course Name and Number: ______________________________

Student Name: ______________________________

Instructor Name: ______________________________

Lab Due Date: ______________________________

Overview

Configure your Windows workstation internal firewall according to the following policy definition. Test and validate your implementation after you configure it based on the policy definition. The following is your workstation internal firewall policy definition:

1. Implement the default Microsoft® Windows internal firewall
2. Add/Block the following additional programs:
   a. Yahoo! Messenger IM Chat
3. Block the following applications:
   a. Telnet
   b. TFTP
   c. SNMP
   d. ICMP echo-request
   e. ICMP echo-reply
4. Allow the following applications under Advanced settings:
   a. FTP
   b. SMTP
   c. POP3
   d. HTTPS
   e. HTTP

LAB #5 – ASSESSMENT WORKSHEET

Configure a Microsoft® Windows Workstation Internal IP Stateful Firewall

Course Name and Number: ____________________

Student Name: ____________________

Instructor Name: ____________________

Lab Due Date: ____________________

Overview

In this lab, you determined the properties and behavior of the default Windows Firewall settings for your workstation, enabled Windows Firewall on the vWorkstation computer, set specific values for blocking or enabling certain transactions, and tested to ensure that Windows Firewall is working properly.

Lab Assessment Questions & Answers

1. Given that the Microsoft® Windows internal firewall is turned on by default, should you disable this firewall if your organization already has a firewall at your LAN-to-WAN domain's Internet ingress/egress point? Why or why not?

____

____

____

____

2. The Microsoft® Windows Firewall inspects within a TCP/IP packet the Layer 4 transport protocol information contained in UDP and TCP. This includes examining the protocol headers and identifying port numbers. What kind of firewall is the Microsoft® Firewall? Explain your answer.

____

____

____

____

3. How do you block specific applications or programs from communicating via TCP/IP from your vWorkstation?

____

____

____

____

4. To configure your internal firewall, you must first identify the applications that you must enable and communicate with throughout your IP network infrastructure. Given the policy definition, identify the port numbers for both the allowed and disallowed applications:

- Telnet Port Number: __________ UDP or TCP
- TFTP Port Number: __________ UDP or TCP
- SNMP Port Number: __________ UDP or TCP
- ICMP echo-request Port Number:__________ UDP or TCP
- ICMP echo-reply Port Number:__________ UDP or TCP
- FTP Port Number:__________ UDP or TCP
- SMTP Port Number:__________ UDP or TCP
- POP3 Port Number:__________ UDP or TCP
- HTTPS Port Number:__________ UDP or TCP
- HTTP Port Number:__________ UDP or TCP

____

____

____

____

5. Where and how do you open the ports and allow specific applications to communicate with your Microsoft® Windows systems?

____

____

____

____

6. What risk exposure are you subjecting your Microsoft® Windows systems to by opening up ports on your internal firewall?

____

____

____

____

7. Explain both the information systems security practitioner and hacker perspectives of using a security scanning application such as Zenmap GUI (Nmap) against a system with an internal firewall enabled.

8. How should you test to determine if your internal firewall configuration is working properly?

9. Define a test plan to test and verify that your internal firewall's open port configurations are working properly.

10. Explain how a layered security strategy can be deployed from the LAN-to-WAN domain, to the LAN domain, and to the Workstation domain with the use of internal firewalls.

Design a De-Militarized Zone (DMZ) for a LAN-to-WAN Ingress/Egress

LAB 6

Introduction

In this lab, you will design a block diagram of a LAN-to-WAN DMZ for a fictitious e-commerce company, Online Goodies, given a list of functional and technical business requirements as well as a set of predefined components. You also will provide a written functional overview and description of how your DMZ and LAN-to-WAN domain security solution meets the defined requirements.

This lab is a paper-based design lab and does not require use of the Virtual Security Cloud Lab (VSCL). To successfully complete the deliverables for this lab, you will need access to a text editor or word processor, such as Microsoft® Word. For some labs, you may also need access to a graphics line drawing application, such as Visio or PowerPoint.

> **Note:**
> If you don't have a word processor or graphics package, use OpenOffice on the student landing vWorkstation for your lab deliverables and to answer the lab assessment questions. To capture screenshots, **press Prt Sc > MSPAINT**, paste into a text document, and **save** the document in the Security_Strategies folder (**C:\Security_Strategies**) using the File Transfer function.

Learning Objectives and Outcomes

Upon completing this lab, you will be able to:

- Review physical and logical requirements for designing a secure LAN-to-WAN domain with an Internet ingress/egress connectivity solution
- Identify common network devices and security appliances needed for the implementation of a DMZ and secure LAN-to-WAN domain infrastructure
- Select the needed physical security appliances to implement a DMZ and secure LAN-to-WAN domain
- Define the logical traffic-filtering schema required for firewalls based on the application connectivity requirements for inbound and outbound traffic
- Design and recommend a layered security solution for remote access to the DMZ and the internal network

Deliverables

Upon completion of this lab, you are required to provide the following deliverables to your instructor:

1. Block diagram of a LAN-to-WAN DMZ;
2. A written function overview of your design;
3. Lab Assessment Questions & Answers for Lab #6.

Hands-On Steps

1. This lab begins with a request from your supervisor. As the newest member of the network administration team for a fictitious e-commerce company, Online Goodies, you will be required to design a LAN-to-WAN DMZ. Your supervisor has provided you with a list of functional and technical business requirements and a sample diagram of a similar system to get you started.

FIGURE 6.1
Functional and technical requirements for the DMZ

Functional and Technical Requirements

- Design to incorporate three zones: Internet zone (outside network), DMZ zone (external servers), private zone (internal network)
- Internet zone must support secure remote access users via VPN clients and IPSec
- Internet zone must include an IP stateful firewall and terminate the remote access VPNs
- DMZ zone must house production Internet services, such as DNS, WWW server, mail servers
- DMZ zone must incorporate IDS/IPS for all IP traffic traversing inbound to the private zone
- DMZ zone must incorporate dual IP stateful firewalls
- Private zone must protect outbound data leakage with a data leakage prevention system for governance and compliance law requirements
- No remote access users are to have access to the internal network
- Remote access users must use IPSec VPN for secure remote communications
- Remote access users may need access to internal network resources
- Internal network users are subject to an AUP restricting the use of their workstations and Internet connection for business purposes only

FIGURE 6.2
Sample physical diagram solution

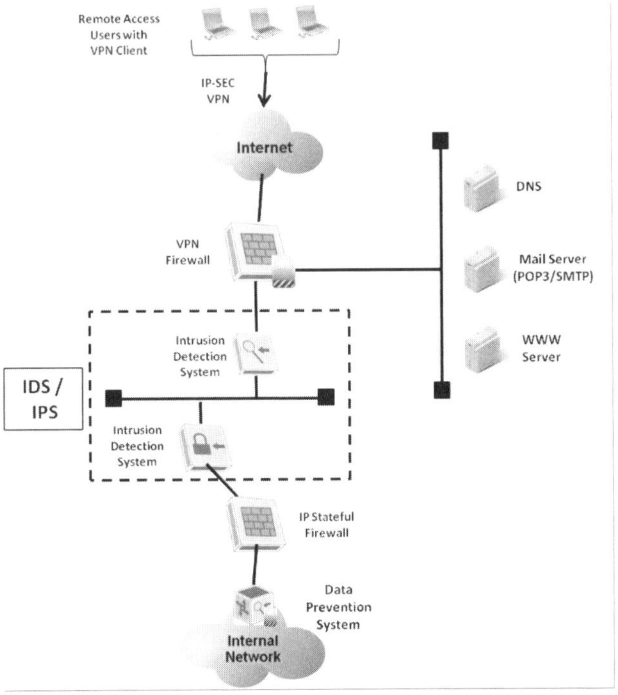

Note:
The next steps will guide you through the steps you will take to complete the deliverables for this lab.

2. From a computer workstation with a graphics line drawing application, such as Visio or PowerPoint, **create** a new document called **LAN-to-WAN DMZ Lab #6**.
3. In your document, **design** a **block diagram** of a LAN-to-WAN DMZ similar to the one in Figure 6.2. Include the following inventory of network and security appliances and devices:
   - IPS
   - Remote users with laptop computers
   - Public Internet
   - VPN firewall
   - DNS
   - IP stateful firewall
   - IDS
   - POP3/SMTP mail servers
   - Content filters
   - E-mail filters and quarantine systems
   - Internal network
   - Data leakage prevention system
   - Ethernet LAN segments (these can be 100Mbps, GigE, etc.)
   - WWW servers
   - E-commerce servers
   - VPN client software

   It is not mandatory to use all of these items as long as the design of your LAN-to-WAN DMZ domain security solution meets the requirements presented in step 1.
4. **Submit** the **text document** to your instructor as a deliverable for this lab.
5. From a computer workstation, **create** a new text document called **DMZ Functional Overview Lab #6**.
6. In your text document, **record** the functional overview of your design and a description of how your DMZ and LAN-to-WAN domain security solution meets the defined requirements.
7. **Submit** the **text document** to your instructor as a deliverable for this lab.

Evaluation Criteria and Rubrics

The following are the evaluation criteria and rubrics for Lab #6 that the students must perform:

1. Was the student able to review physical and logical requirements for designing a secure LAN-to-WAN domain with an Internet ingress/egress connectivity solution? – **[20%]**
2. Was the student able to identify common network devices and security appliances needed for the implementation of a DMZ and secure LAN-to-WAN domain infrastructure? – **[20%]**
3. Was the student able to select the needed physical security appliances to implement a DMZ and secure LAN-to-WAN domain? – **[20%]**
4. Was the student able to define the logical traffic-filtering schema required for firewalls based on the application connectivity requirements for inbound and outbound traffic? – **[20%]**
5. Was the student able to design and recommend a layered security solution for remote access to the DMZ and the internal network? – **[20%]**

LAB #6 – ASSESSMENT WORKSHEET

Design a De-Militarized Zone (DMZ) for a LAN-to-WAN Ingress/Egress

Course Name and Number: ____________________

Student Name: ____________________

Instructor Name: ____________________

Lab Due Date: ____________________

Overview

In this lab, you designed a block diagram of a LAN-to-WAN DMZ for a fictitious e-commerce company, Online Goodies, given a list of functional and technical business requirements as well as a set of predefined components. You also provided a written functional overview and description of how your DMZ and LAN-to-WAN domain security solution meets the defined requirements.

Lab Assessment Questions & Answers

1. Describe how creating zones is helpful in the design of a DMZ and security solution for the LAN-to-WAN domain.

2. How many zones does your design incorporate? Do you think an additional zone may be needed if the e-commerce server were implemented? Explain why or why not.

3. While supporting IPSec VPNs provide a secure, remote access solution for mobile employees, they do not scale and require stringent security operations and management procedures. What alternatives would you recommend for a scalable remote access VPN solution for your design?

4. As per the functional and technical requirements, where must you terminate the VPN tunnels for remote access users?

5. Where would you put an e-mail filter and quarantine system to scan and monitor e-mails and e-mail attachments? Explain why.

6. Where would you put a content filter system to prevent employees from non-business use of the Internet connection? Explain why.

7. Explain how your IDS/IPS positioning and solution achieves the CIA goals of the internal network.

8. Explain how the risk of data leakage can be mitigated with a data leakage prevention system and security monitoring controls.

9. Your organization is under governance and compliance law requirements for protecting customer privacy data and implementing proper security controls to protect that data contained within the internal network. How many security controls does your DMZ and LAN-to-WAN domain design incorporate? List them and describe how they help achieve CIA for your overall solution.

10. What is the cost benefit tradeoff for having this many security controls within the LAN-to-WAN domain? Do you think this is overkill or just right, given the functional and technical requirements definition?

Implement a VPN Tunnel Between a Microsoft® Server and Microsoft® Client

LAB 7

Introduction

In this lab, you will set up a virtual private network (VPN) tunnel between a Windows server and client computers using RADIUS (Remote Authentication Dial-in User Service) authentication.

Learning Objectives

Upon completing this lab, you will be able to:

- Configure a Microsoft® server with RADIUS authentication for secure remote access from Microsoft® clients
- Configure a remote access connection using a virtual private network (VPN) between the Microsoft® server and Microsoft® client
- Apply a new RADIUS authentication definition for remote access on a Microsoft® client workstation
- Apply remote access permissions for a Microsoft® client using RADIUS authentication
- Verify remote access to the Microsoft® server from the Microsoft® client and enable Wireshark to verify/validate encrypted IP transmissions

TOOLS AND SOFTWARE

NAME	MORE INFORMATION
Microsoft® Windows Network Policy Server (NPS)	http://technet.microsoft.com/en-us/network/bb629414.aspx
Wireshark	http://www.wireshark.org

Deliverables

Upon completion of this lab, you are required to provide the following deliverables to your instructor:

1. Wireshark PCAP file showing encrypted IP communications between the Microsoft server and Microsoft® client;
2. Lab Assessment Questions & Answers for Lab #7.

Hands-On Steps

1. This lab begins at the student landing vWorkstation virtual machine desktop of the VSCL, as shown here.

FIGURE 7.1

"Student Landing" VSCL workstation

> **Note:**
> The next steps will open the remote desktop connection to the Windows Server 2008 and install network services.

2. To open the Windows Server 2008, **double-click** the **ISSA_VM Server Farm_RDP icon** on the desktop.
3. **Double-click** the **Targetw2k8b.rdp file**.

FIGURE 7.2

Open a remote desktop connection to the Windows Server 2008

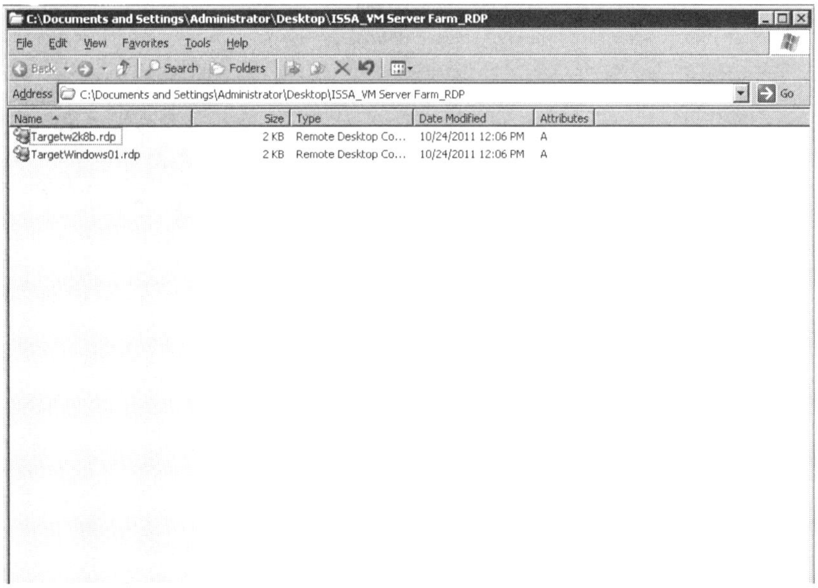

4. In the Remote Desktop Connection Security Warning dialog box, **click** the **Don't prompt me again for connections to this remote computer checkbox**.

FIGURE 7.3
Remote Desktop Connection Security Warning dialog box

5. **Click OK** to close the dialog box.
   This dialog box loads automatically when this connection is opened.
6. **Click** the **WIN2K8B\Administrator icon** on the Windows server desktop.

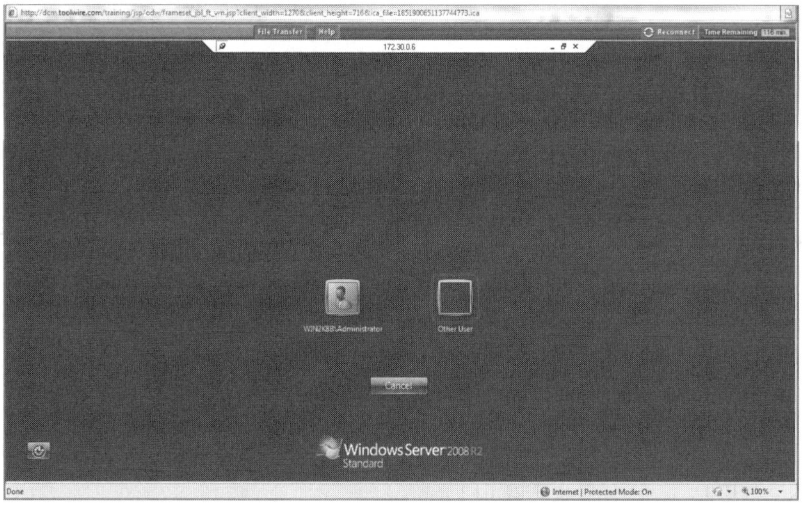

FIGURE 7.4
Windows Server 2008 logon screen

7. **Log on** to **Targetw2k8b** with the following credentials:
   - Username: **Administrator**
   - Password: **ISS316Security**
8. From the Windows server, **click** the **Windows Start button**.

9. **Select Administrative Tools** from the menu.
10. **Click Server Manager**.
11. Use the scroll bar at the right of the Server Manager to locate the Roles Summary heading and **click Add Roles** in the right-hand pane. The Add Roles Wizard will launch.
12. **Click Next** to skip the Before You Begin screen.
13. On the Select Server Roles screen, **click the Network Policy and Access Services checkbox**.

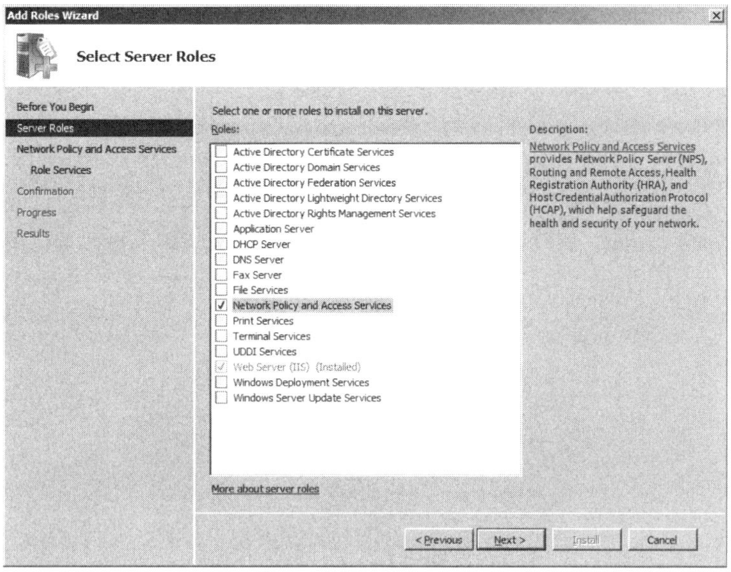

FIGURE 7.5

Add Windows Server Network Policy and Access Services

14. **Click Next**.
15. Review the Network Policy and Access Services screen and **click Next** again.
16. On the Select Role Services screen, **click** the following checkboxes and **click Next** to continue:
    - **Network Policy Server**
    - **Routing and Remote Access Services**

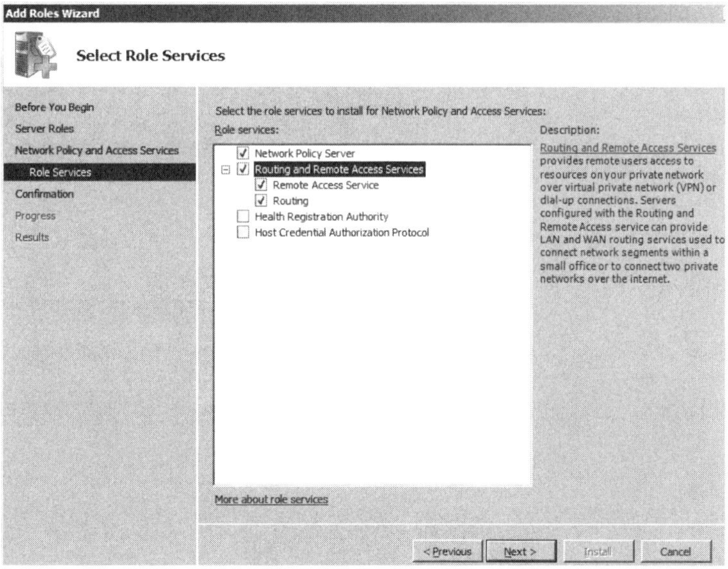

FIGURE 7.6

Add Windows Server Routing and Remote Access Services

The checkboxes for Remote Access Service and Routing will be checked automatically when the Routing and Remote Access Services checkbox is selected.

17. At the Confirm Installation Selections screen, **click Install** to install the selected services.
18. **Click Close** to close the Add Roles Wizard.

> **Note:**
> The next steps will enable the Remote Access Connection Manager Service.

19. **Click Roles** in the left-hand pane of the Windows Server Manager.

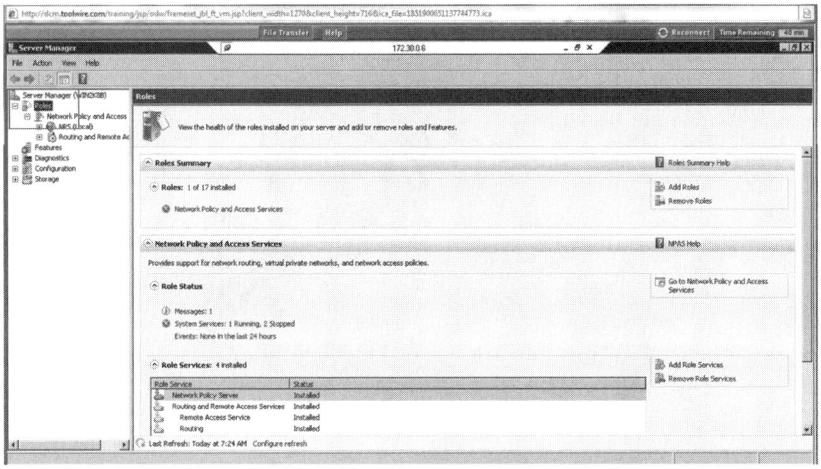

FIGURE 7.7
Windows Server Manager Roles screen

20. **Click Network Policy and Access Services** under the Roles Summary header in the right-hand pane.
21. Use the scroll bar at the right of the Server Manager to locate the System Services heading and **click Remote Access Connection Manager**.
22. **Click Start** in the box to the right of the System Services header.

The status of the Remote Access Connection Manager is now changed to Running.

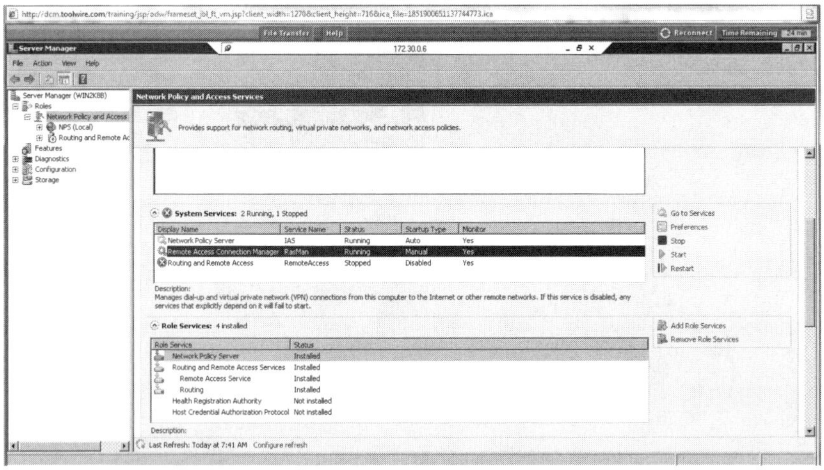

FIGURE 7.8
Remote Access Connection Manager service is running

23. **Close** the **Windows Server Manager**.

> **Note:**
> The next steps will use RADIUS to configure a virtual private network (VPN).

24. **Click** the **Windows Start button**.
25. **Select Administrative Tools** from the menu.
26. **Click Network Policy Server** to open the application.
27. In the Standard Configuration drop-down menu, **select RADIUS server for Dial-Up or VPN Connections**. The RADIUS configuration options populate the screen below the drop-down menu.
28. **Click Configure VPN or Dial-Up**.

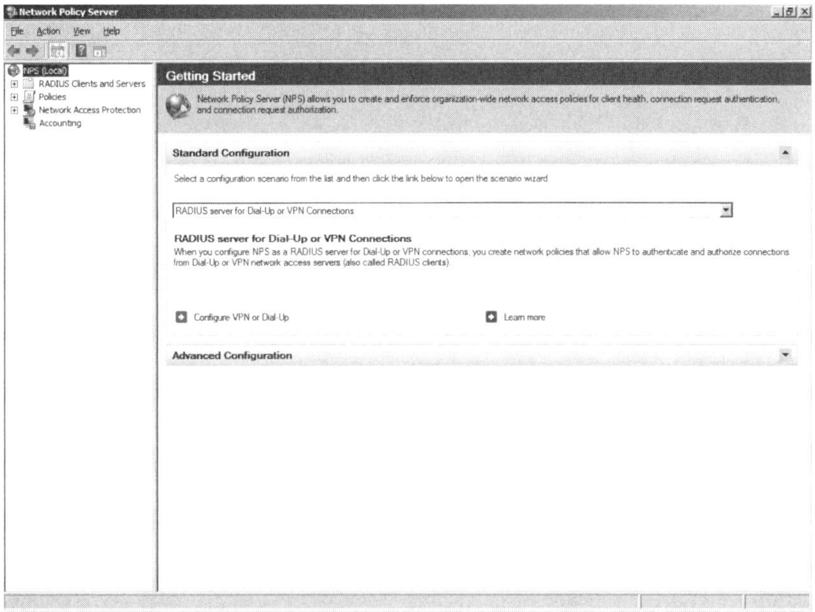

FIGURE 7.9
Configure a VPN

29. In the Configure VPN or Dial-Up dialog box, **click** the **Virtual Private Network (VPN) Connections radio button**.

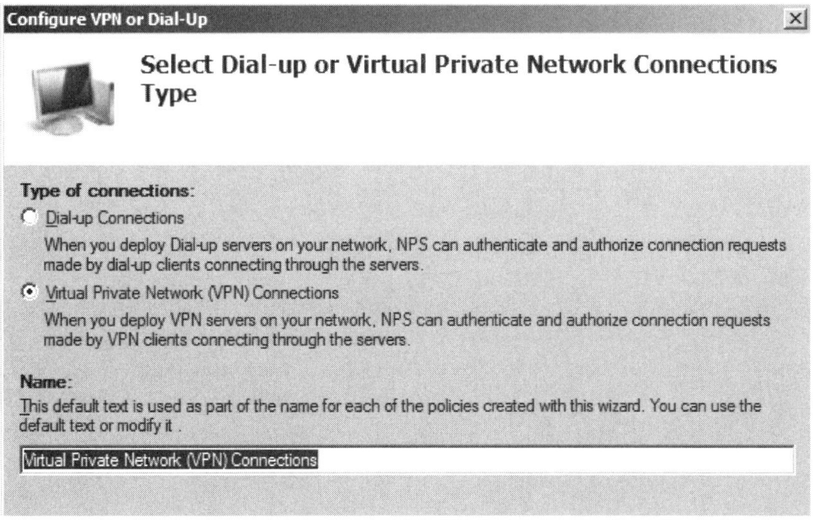

FIGURE 7.10
Configure virtual private network

30. **Click Next** to accept the default name for this VPN.
31. **Click Next** to skip the Specify Dial-Up or VPN Server screen.
32. At the Configure Authentication Methods screen, **click** the **Microsoft Encrypted Authentication version 2 (MS-CHAPv2) checkbox**.

FIGURE 7.11

Configuring RADIUS authentication methods

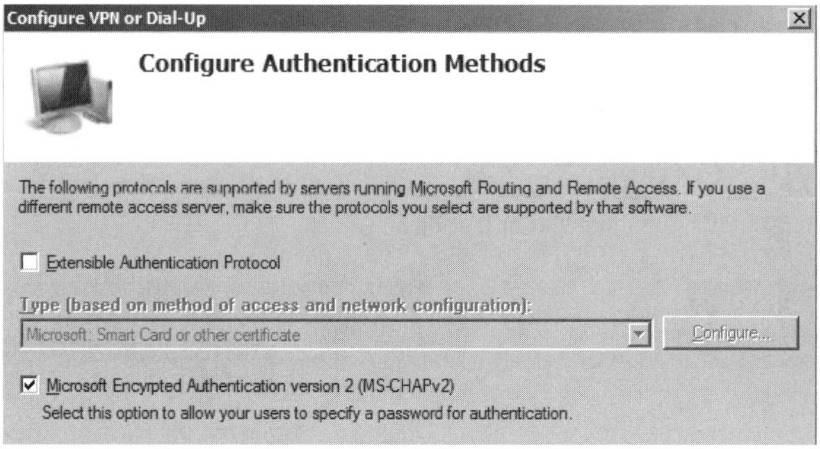

33. **Click Next.**
34 **Click Next** to skip the Specify User Groups screen.
35. **Click Next** to skip the Specify IP Filters screen.
36. On the Specify Encryption Settings screen, **click** the checkboxes labeled:
    - **Basic encryption (MPPE 40-bit)**
    - **Strong encryption (MPPE 56-bit)**
    - **Strongest encryption (MPPE 128-bit)**

FIGURE 7.12

Configure VPN encryption settings and strength

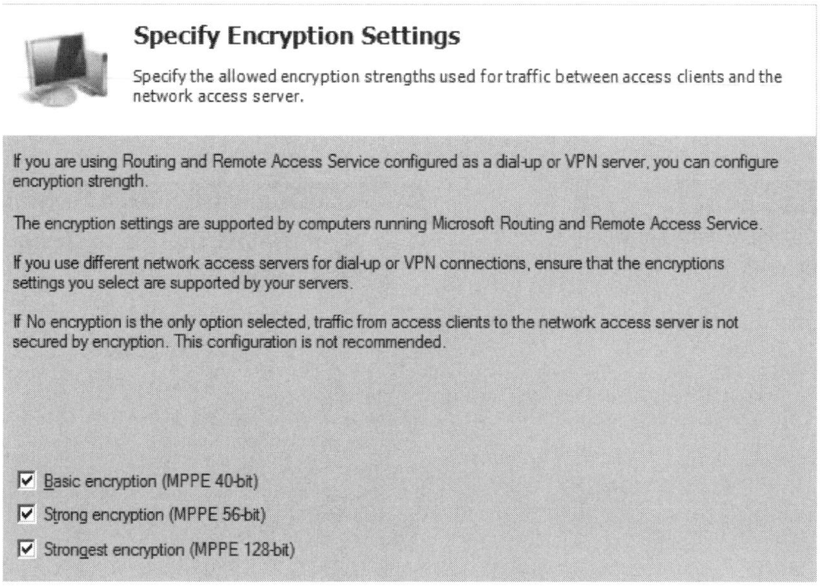

37. **Click Next** to skip the Specify a Realm Name screen.
38. **Click Finish** to complete the VPN/RADIUS configuration.

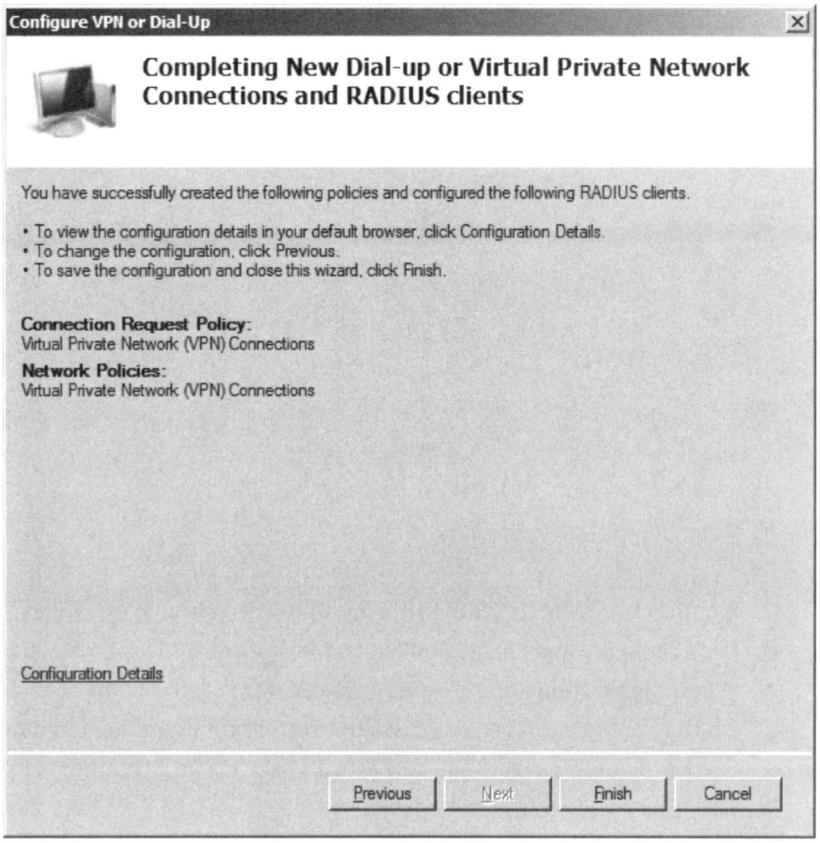

FIGURE 7.13
Completing RADIUS implementation

39. **Close** the **Network Policy Server application**.

Note:
The next steps will use RADIUS to launch a Routing and Remote Access service.

40. **Click** the **Windows Start button**.
41. **Select Administrative Tools** from the menu.

42. **Click Routing and Remote Access.**

FIGURE 7.14

Routing and Remote Access management console

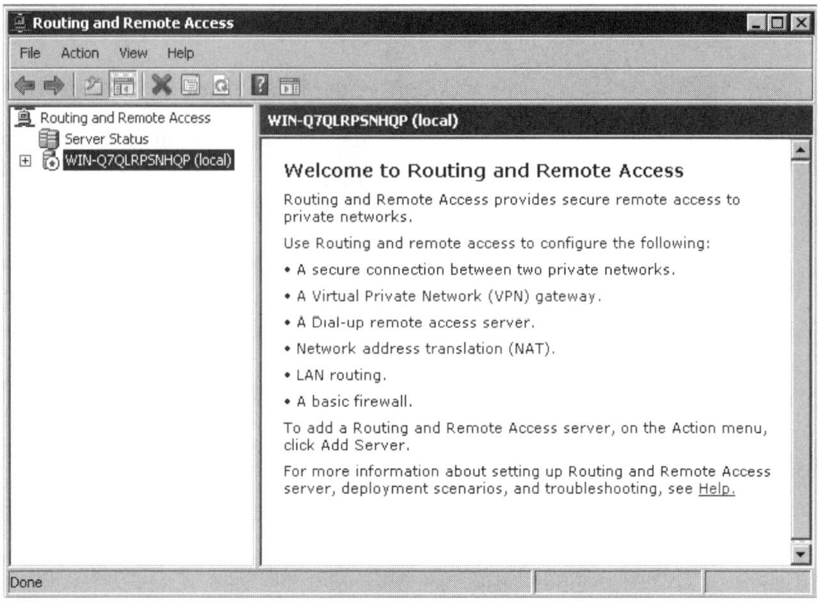

43. **Right-click** on **WIN-Q7QLRPSNHQP (local)** (the machine name for WIN2K8B) in the left pane.
44. **Click Configure and Enable Routing and Remote Access** from the shortcut menu.
45. When the Routing and Remote Access Server Setup Wizard opens, **click Next.**
46. On the Configuration screen, **click** the **Custom configuration radio button** and **click Next.**
47. On the next screen, **click the VPN access checkbox** and **click Next** to continue.
48. **Click Finish** to close the wizard.

FIGURE 7.15

Completing the Routing and Remote Access Server Setup Wizard

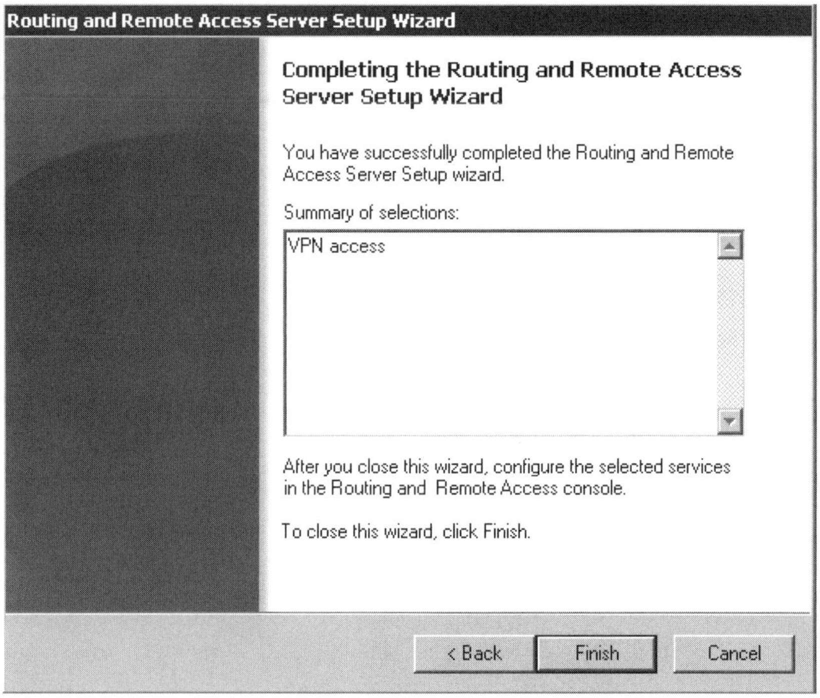

49. **Click OK** on both Routing and Remote Access confirmation messages.
50. **Click Start service** when prompted.

FIGURE 7.16

Starting the Routing and Remote Access service

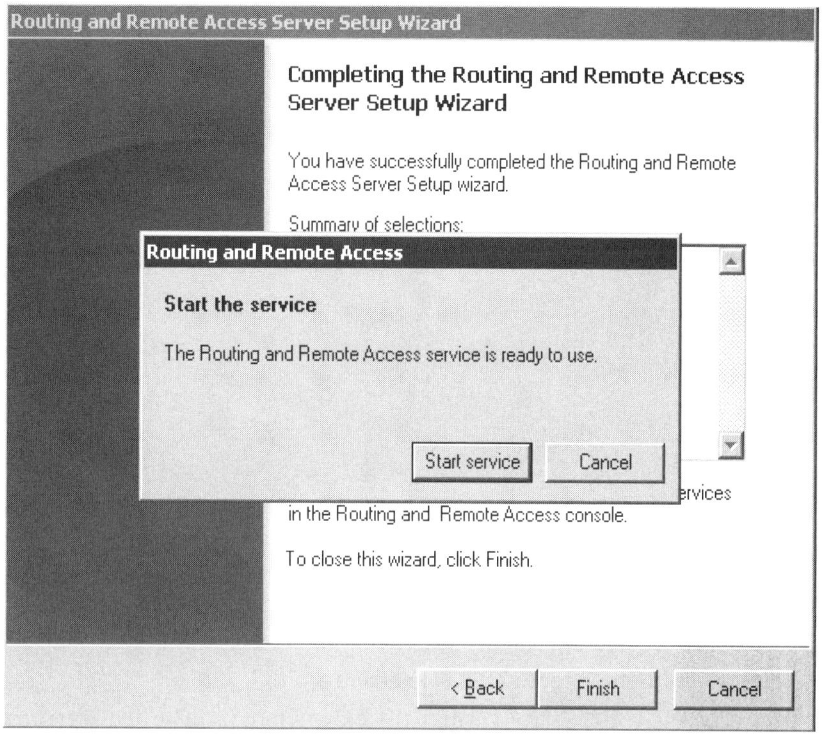

The Routing and Remote Access management console will populate the options below the WIN-Q7QLRPSNHQP server directory in the left pane.

51. **Right-click** on **WIN-Q7QLRPSNHQP (local)** in the left pane.
52. **Click Properties** on the shortcut menu.
53. **Click** the **IPv4 tab** in the Properties dialog box.
54. **Select** the **Static address pool radio button**.

55. **Click Add** and enter the following IP address range in the New IPv4 Address Range dialog box:
    - Start IP address: **172.30.0.250**
    - End IP address: **172.30.0.252**
56. **Click OK** to close the New IPv4 Address Range dialog box.

FIGURE 7.17

Set an IP address range for remote connections

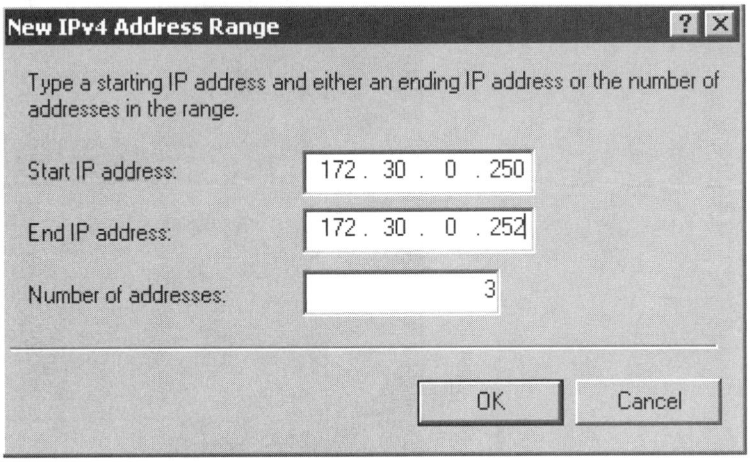

57. **Close** the **Routing and Remote Access window**.
58. **Minimize** the **Targetw2k8b connection**.

    The ISSA_VM Server Farm_RDP folder should still be open on the vWorkstation desktop.

> **Note:**
> The next steps will open a different computer to test the VPN connection you just configured.

59. **Double-click** the **TargetWindows01.rdp file** to open the Windows server.
60. **Log on** to **TargetWindows01** using the following credentials:
    - User name: **Administrator**
    - Password: **ISS316Security**

61. To launch the New Connection Wizard, **click** the **Windows Start button**.
62. **Select Settings** from the menu.
63. **Click Network Connections.**
64. **Double-click** on the **New Connection Wizard icon**.

FIGURE 7.18

New Connection Wizard

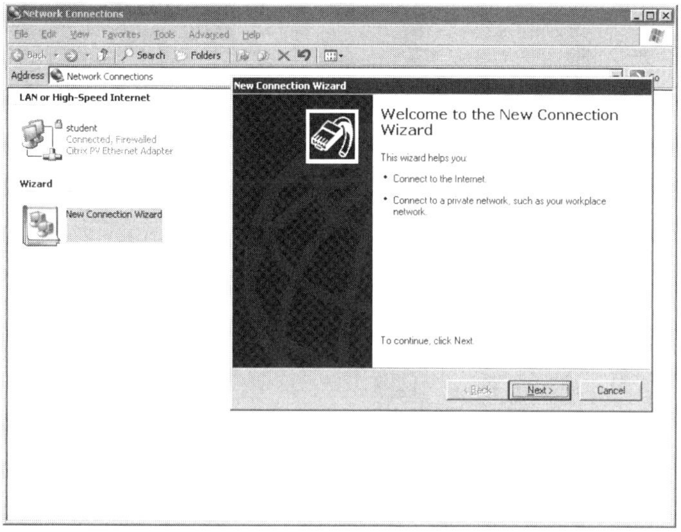

65. **Click Next** to skip the welcome screen.
66. At the Network Connection Type screen, **select** the **Connect to the network at my workplace radio button** and **click Next.**
67. At the Network Connection screen, **click** the **Virtual Private Network Connection radio button** and **click Next**.
68. At the Connection Name screen, **type VLABS** in the Company Name box.
69. **Click Next** to continue.
70. At the VPN Server Selection screen, **type 172.30.0.6** (the IP address for the WIN2K8B RADIUS server) and **click Next** to continue.

FIGURE 7.19

Enter RADIUS server address for VPN

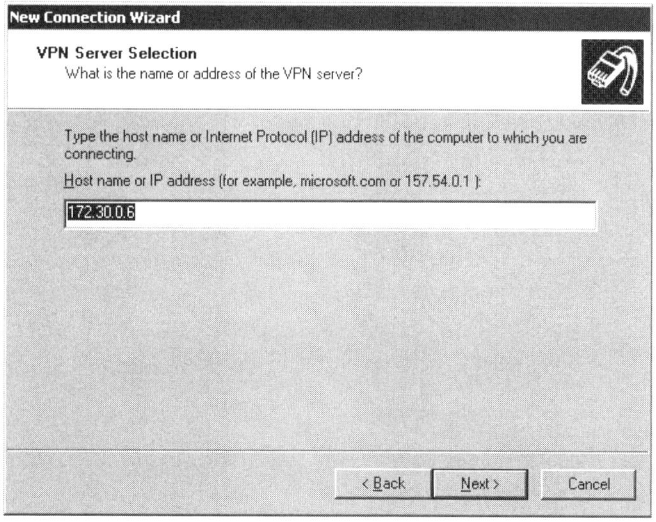

71. At the Connection Availability screen, **click** the **Anyone's use radio button** and **click Next** to continue.
72. **Click** the **Add a shortcut to this connection to my desktop checkbox** and **click Finish** to complete the New Connection Wizard.

FIGURE 7.20

Complete the New Connection Wizard

Note:
The Connect VLABS log on dialog box will open when the New Connection Wizard closes. This is the screen through which you will connect to the VPN. However, it is important that you start Wireshark on TargetWindows01 *before* connecting to the VPN. The next steps will use Wireshark to capture and analyze network traffic between client and server.

73. **Double-click** on the **Wireshark icon** on the TargetWindows01 desktop to launch the application.

FIGURE 7.21

TargetWindows01 desktop

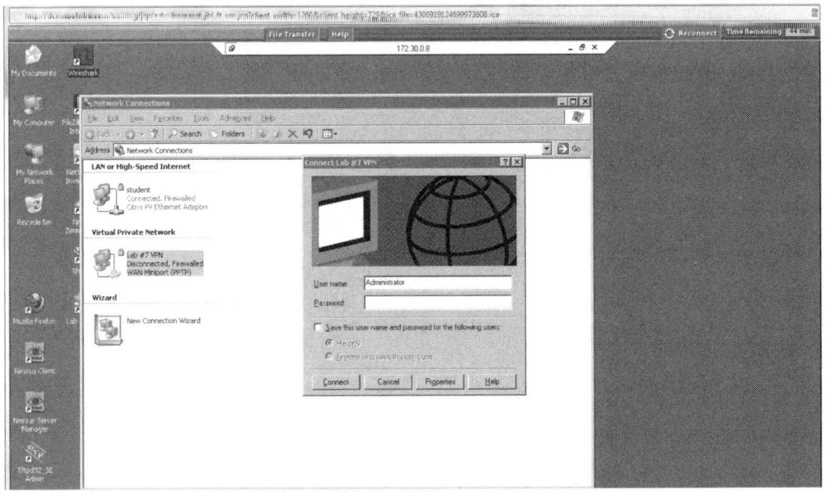

74. **Click** the **Citrix Systems link** in the Interface List section of the Wireshark welcome screen to start the packet capture.
75. **Minimize** the **Wireshark window**.
76. **Type** the following logon credentials in the **Connect VLABS dialog box**:
    - User name: **Administrator**
    - Password: **ISS316Security**

FIGURE 7.22

Connect to the WIN2K8B VPN

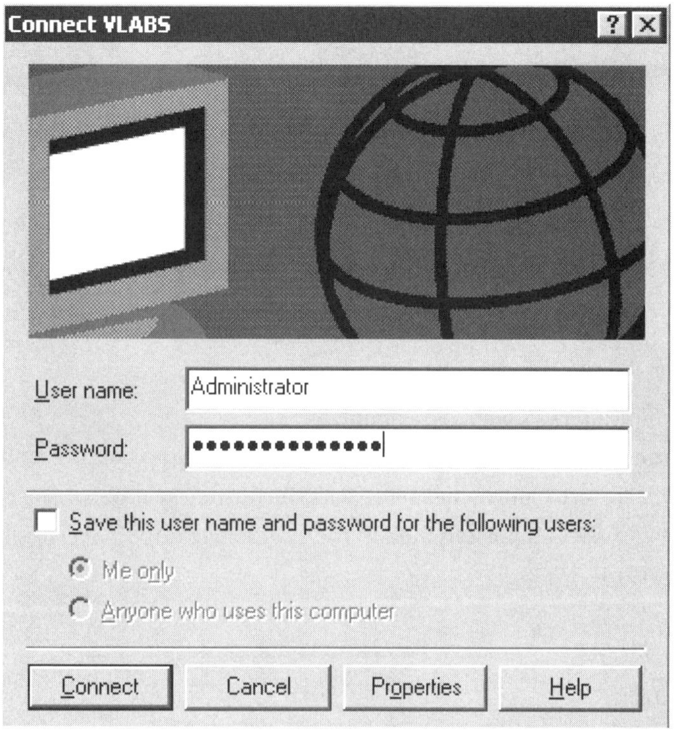

77. **Click Connect** and verify that the connection was successfully established. A message will appear in the Windows system tray.

> **Note:**
> The next steps will explore the WIN2K8B server through the VPN connection you established earlier.

78. From the vWorkstation desktop, **click** the **Windows Start button**.
79. **Select Run** from the menu.
80. **Type cmd** in the dialog box and **click OK**.

81. In the Windows Command Prompt window, **type ipconfig /all** and **press Enter**.
Verify the IP address assignment from the VPN/RADIUS server.

FIGURE 7.23

Verify IP address of VPN server

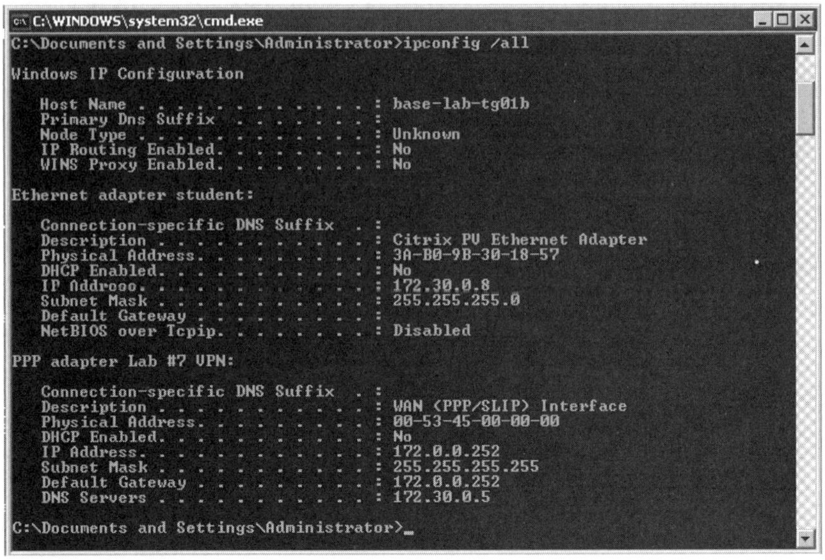

82. **Close** the **Windows Command Prompt**.
83. **Maximize** the Wireshark application and click the **Stop Capture icon** to stop the capture.
84. **Click** the **Protocol column header** to sort the output by protocol type.
85. **Find PPP COMP Compressed Data** in the Protocol column to verify your client-server VPN connection is encrypted.

FIGURE 7.24

VPN encrypted traffic verified by Wireshark

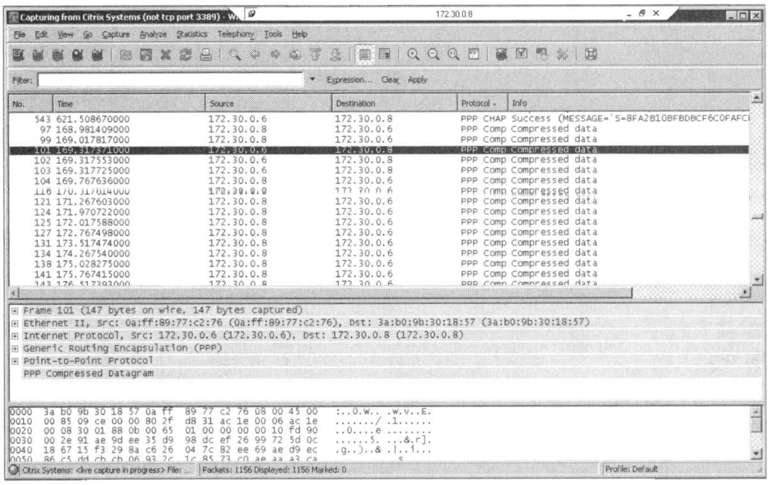

86. **Click** the **Save icon** and **use** the following information to save the scan to the TargetWindows01 desktop:
   - Save in: **Desktop**
   - File name: **Lab #7.pcap**
   - Save as type: **Wireshark/tcpdump/… - libpcap (*.pcap, *.cap)**
87. **Close** the **TargetWindows01 session** to return to the vWorkstation desktop.
88. Use the **File Transfer button** on the vWorkstation desktop to transfer the document to your physical workstation.

Evaluation Criteria and Rubrics

The following are the evaluation criteria and rubrics for Lab #7 that the students must perform:

1. Was the student able to configure a Microsoft® server with RADIUS authentication for secure remote access from Microsoft® clients? – [**20%**]
2. Was the student able to configure a remote access connection using a virtual private network (VPN) between the Microsof® server and Microsoft® client? – [**20%**]
3. Was the student able to apply a new RADIUS authentication definition for remote access for a Microsoft® client workstation? – [**20%**]
4. Was the student able to apply remote access permissions for a Microsoft® client using RADIUS authentication? – [**20%**]
5. Was the student able to verify remote access to the Microsoft® server from the Microsoft® client and enable Wireshark to verify/validate encrypted IP transmissions? – [**20%**]

LAB #7 – ASSESSMENT WORKSHEET

Implement a VPN Tunnel Between a Microsoft® Server and Microsoft® Client

Course Name and Number: ______________________________

Student Name: ______________________________

Instructor Name: ______________________________

Lab Due Date: ______________________________

Overview

This lab presented how to design, configure, and test a remote access solution using VPN technology to secure and encrypt the end-to-end IP packet transmissions from a VPN client workstation to the VPN server. This lab demonstrated how to configure a secure remote access solution using an IPSec VPN.

Lab Assessment Questions & Answers

1. What is the name of the Windows Sever 2008 role you need to deploy to provide remote access services to clients? Explain why this service is important in a corporate environment.

____

____

____

____

2. What was the IP host range that was allocated for the remote VPN client pool?

____

____

____

____

3. How many encryption settings are available from the remote access server? Which one is best? Which one provides backward compatibility?

____

____

____

____

4. During a remote access session, how many times is a client asked to provide credentials? Is this an example of multi-factor authentication? Explain.

5. Why is it important to use strong encryption in both authentication and communication protocols? Explain.

6. Name the available authentication methods (protocols) available in Microsoft® Windows Server 2008. Which authentication method is considered stronger? Why?

7. What other type of connections are supported by Microsoft® Remote Access services in Server 2008?

8. After connecting to the VPN server, which IP address from the pool was assigned to the client? Aside from the IPCONFIG command, how else can you verify IP settings on a Windows workstation?

9. How can you verify that the IPSec VPN tunnel is encrypting your IP data payload?

10. What kind of encryption was used for your remote access VPN connection between the remote access server and the client?

Design a Layered Security Strategy for an IP Network Infrastructure

LAB 8

Introduction

In this lab, you will design a layered security strategy, similar to the seven domains of a typical IT infrastructure, for the Cisco Mock IT infrastructure shown in Figure 8.2. You will base your design on a set of functional and technical requirements. You also will provide a written functional overview and description of how your security strategy meets the defined requirements.

This lab is a paper-based design lab and does not require use of the Virtual Security Cloud Lab (VSCL). To successfully complete the deliverables for this lab, you will need access to a text editor or word processor, such as Microsoft® Word. For some labs, you may also need access to a graphics line drawing application, such as Visio or PowerPoint.

> **Note:**
> If you don't have a word processor or graphics package, use OpenOffice on the student landing vWorkstation for your lab deliverables and to answer the lab assessment questions. To capture screenshots, press **Prt Sc > MSPAINT**, paste into a text document, and **save** the document in the Security_Strategies folder (**C:\Security_Strategies**) using the File Transfer function.

Learning Objectives and Outcomes

Upon completing this lab, you will be able to:

- Review the physical and logical implementation of the classroom Mock IT infrastructure, which comprises the Cisco core WAN, Cisco 2811 routers, Cisco 2960 layer 3 switches, ASA 5505s, and the virtualized server farm
- Review the functional and technical requirements for designing a layered security solution for the physical and logical IT infrastructure and select appropriate network devices and security appliances needed for the implementation
- Align firewall configuration parameters to inbound and outbound IP protocols servicing various applications
- Integrate the secure DMZ solution into an overall layered security strategy for the Mock IT infrastructure
- Design a layered security strategy for the classroom Mock IT infrastructure

Deliverables

Upon completion of this lab, you are required to provide the following deliverables to your instructor:

1. Block diagram design of a layered security solution;
2. A written function overview of your design;
3. Lab Assessment Questions & Answers for Lab #8.

Hands-On Steps

1. This lab begins with a request from your supervisor. As the newest member of the network administration team for a fictitious e-commerce company, Online Goodies, you will be required to design a block diagram of a layered security solution, similar to the seven domains of a typical IT infrastructure. Your supervisor has provided you with a list of functional and technical business requirements and a diagram of the CISCO Mock IT infrastructure to get you started.

FIGURE 8.1

Functional and technical requirements for the block diagram

Functional and Technical Requirements

- Internet must support secure remote access solution
- DMZ is required for external servers, applications for remote access from the Internet
- Internal server farm contains privacy data and compliance requirements
- Client wants to implement an e-commerce server and application in the future
- Remote users in the five designated cities require access to mail server but are not to have access to the server farm servers, applications, or data
- Remote users in the five designated cities have their own local servers, applications, and data that require secure file transfers between the remote server and the server farm for nightly batch processing
- Departmental users connected to LAN Switch 1 and LAN Switch 2 on departmental VLANs. Users within a department need to access the shared mail servers and their respective servers and applications on the server farm but only their own
- The organization shares its dedicated Internet WAN connection on the ASA_Student for the five designated cities and remote locations
- The organization has an AUP and monitors employee use of e-mail and WWW surfing
- The organization wants to protect against unauthorized access and maintain compliance by securing and maintaining confidentiality for customer privacy data

FIGURE 8.2

CISCO Mock IT infrastructure

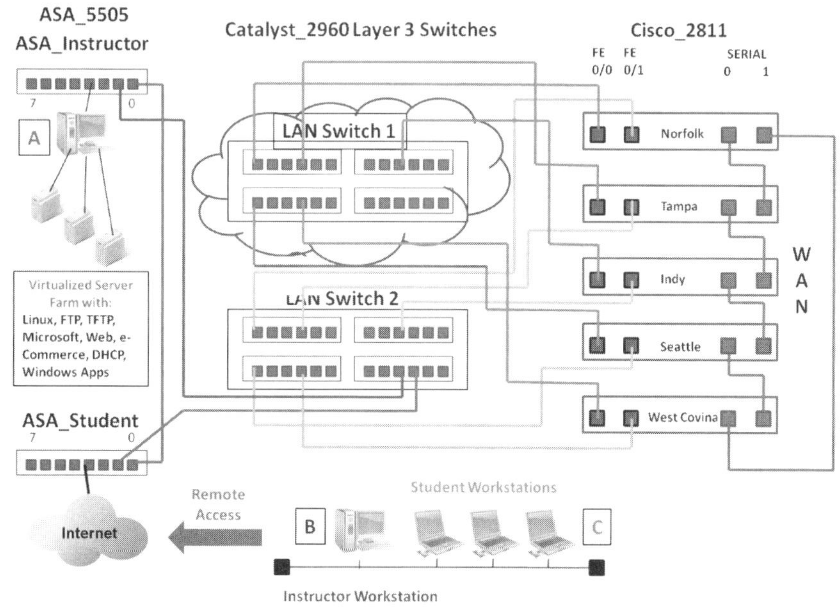

> **Note:**
> The next steps will guide you through the steps you will take to complete the deliverables for this lab.

2. From a computer workstation with a graphics line drawing application, such as Visio or PowerPoint, **create** a new document called **Layered Security Strategy Lab #8**.
3. In your document, **design** a **block diagram** of a layered security strategy, similar to the seven domains of a typical IT infrastructure.
4. In your diagram, **number each block** on your diagram.
5. **Submit** the **text document** to your instructor as a deliverable for this lab.
6. From a computer workstation, **create** a new text document called **Functional Overview of Layered Security Strategy Lab #8**.
7. In your text document, **record** the functional overview of your layered security solution describing each block in your diagram. Explain your security controls and the security countermeasures you are enabling for each block in your diagram.
8. **Submit** the **text document** to your instructor as a deliverable for this lab.

Evaluation Criteria and Rubrics

The following are the evaluation criteria and rubrics for Lab #8 that the students must perform:

1. Was the student able to review the physical and logical implementation of the classroom Mock IT infrastructure, which comprises the Cisco core WAN, Cisco 2811 routers, Cisco 2960 layer 3 switches, ASA 5505s, and the virtualized server farm? – **[20%]**
2. Was the student able to review the functional and technical requirements for designing a layered security solution for the physical and logical IT infrastructure and select appropriate network devices and security appliances needed for the implementation? – **[20%]**
3. Was the student able to align firewall configuration parameters to inbound and outbound IP protocols servicing various applications? – **[20%]**
4. Was the student able to integrate his/her secure DMZ solution into an overall layered security strategy for the Mock IT infrastructure? – **[20%]**
5. Was the student able to design a layered security strategy for the classroom Mock IT infrastructure? – **[20%]**

LAB #8 – ASSESSMENT WORKSHEET

Design a Layered Security Strategy for an IP Network Infrastructure

Course Name and Number: ______________________

Student Name: ______________________

Instructor Name: ______________________

Lab Due Date: ______________________

Overview

In this lab, you designed a layered security strategy, similar to the seven domains of a typical IT infrastructure, for the Cisco Mock IT infrastructure shown in Figure 8.2. You based your design on a set of functional and technical requirements. You also provided a written functional overview and description of how your security strategy meets the defined requirements.

Lab Assessment Questions & Answers

1. Explain why a layered security strategy helps mitigate risk and threats both external and internal.

____

____

____

____

2. Why is it a good idea to put shared servers and services on a DMZ when both internal and external users need access?

____

____

____

____

3. What recommendations do you have for the future e-commerce server and deployment in regard to physical location and backend security for privacy data and credit card data?

4. What recommendations do you have to secure the server farm from unauthorized access?

5. If the organization implemented wireless LAN (WLAN) technology, what would you recommend regarding the use of VPNs or encryption within the internal network when accessing the server farm?

6. What is the purpose of a proxy server on a DMZ?

7. What is the purpose of an IDS/IPS on a DMZ?

8. Where should the IDS/IPS be located on the DMZ and why?

9. What servers or services can you install on the public-facing side of your DMZ?

10. Do you need a firewall in a router enabled if you have an external IP stateful firewall?

Construct a Linux Host Firewall and Monitor for IP Traffic

LAB 9

Introduction

In this lab, you will configure the Gufw Ubuntu host IP stateful firewall as an internal service running on the Linux desktop. By defining what IP traffic is allowed and what IP traffic is denied, you can implement another layer of security in your overall layered security strategy. In addition, you will explore some useful network management and security operation tools, which can be enabled to monitor your IP traffic and security functions.

Learning Objectives

Upon completing this lab, you will be able to:

- List the features and functions of Gufw, an Ubuntu Linux desktop internal host firewall
- Document an Ubuntu Linux internal IP stateful firewall with default configuration settings
- Configure the Ubuntu Linux internal IP stateful firewall as per policy definition
- Monitor IP traffic using applications and tools on a TargetUbuntu server for specific kinds of IP, UDP, or TCP traffic
- Test and verify the internal host firewall implementation on the Ubuntu Linux desktop, and monitor IP traffic on a TargetUbuntu server

TOOLS AND SOFTWARE

NAME	MORE INFORMATION
DVWA	http://www.dvwa.co.uk
Gufw	http://help.ubuntu.com/community/Gufw
Bmon	http://www.infradead.org/~tgr/bmon/
Iftop	http://linux.die.net/man/8/iftop/
Pktstat	http://taufanlubis.wordpress.com/2008/01/03/network-monitor-pktstat/
Iperf	http://sourceforge.net/projects/iperf/
Tcptrack	http://linux.die.net/man/1/tcptrack/

Deliverables

Upon completion of this lab, you are required to provide the following deliverables to your instructor:

1. A text document that includes screen captures of the following items:
   - The changes made to the TargetUbuntu Linux internal firewall configuration;
   - The changes made to the firewall configuration file;
   - The output generated by the IP monitoring tools used in this lab;
   - The output confirming that the firewall changes were configured properly;
2. Lab Assessment Questions & Answers for Lab #9.

Hands-On Steps

1. This lab begins at the student landing vWorkstation virtual machine desktop of the VSCL, as shown here.

FIGURE 9.1
"Student Landing" VSCL workstation

> **Note:**
> The next steps open a remote desktop connection to the TargetUbuntu01 virtual machine and change the security settings for the Damn Vulnerable Web App (DVWA).

2. **Double-click** the **ISSA_VM Server Farm_RDP icon** on the desktop.
3. **Double-click** the **TargetUbuntu01 file** to open a remote desktop connection to the Linux Server.

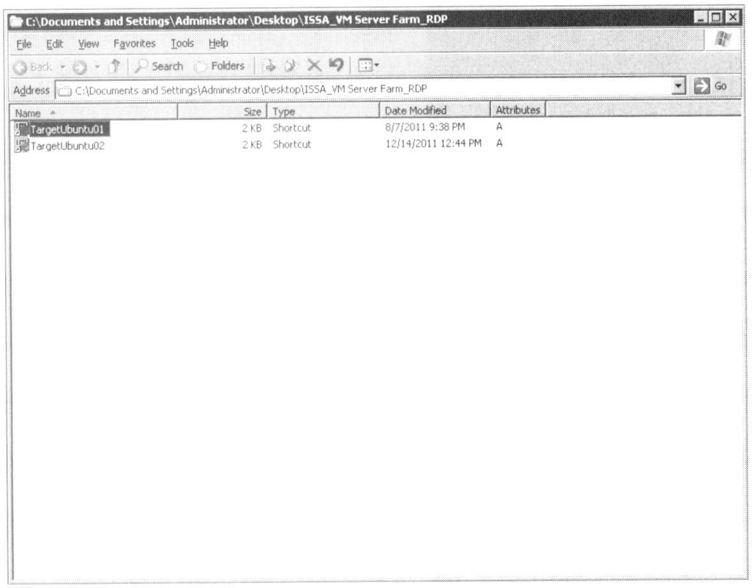

FIGURE 9.2
Connect to the TargetUbuntu01 server

4. **Log in** to the **TargetUbuntu01 VM** server with the following credentials:
    - User name: **student**
    - Password: **ISS316Security**
5. From the Linux toolbar, **click Applications, click Accessories,** and **select Terminal** to open the Linux command prompt.
6. Type **ifconfig -a** to verify the IP address (inet addr) for this computer.

FIGURE 9.3
Verifying the IP address

7. **Document** the **IP address** (inetaddr=________________________) you find in the eth0 section of the Terminal window. You will need it to connect to the Damn Vulnerable Web Application (DVWA) later in this lab.
8. **Close** the **Terminal window**.
9. **Minimize** the **TargetUbuntu01 window**. You will use this again later.

> **Note:**
> The next steps open a remote desktop connection to the TargetUbuntu02 virtual machine and configure the internal firewall based on a predefined policy definition. You will document this configuration in a text document and submit it as a deliverable for this lab.

10. **Double-click** the **TargetUbuntu02 file** to open a remote desktop connection to the virtual machine.
11. **Log in** to the **TargetUbuntu02** machine with the following credentials:
    - User name: **student**
    - Password: **ISS316Security**

12. From the Linux toolbar, **click System**, **click Administration**, and **select Firewall configuration**.
13. In the Firewall dialog box, **click** the **Firewall enabled checkbox** in the top right corner to turn on the firewall.
14. **Click** the **Deny incoming traffic radio button** in the Current Configuration section of the dialog box, if necessary.

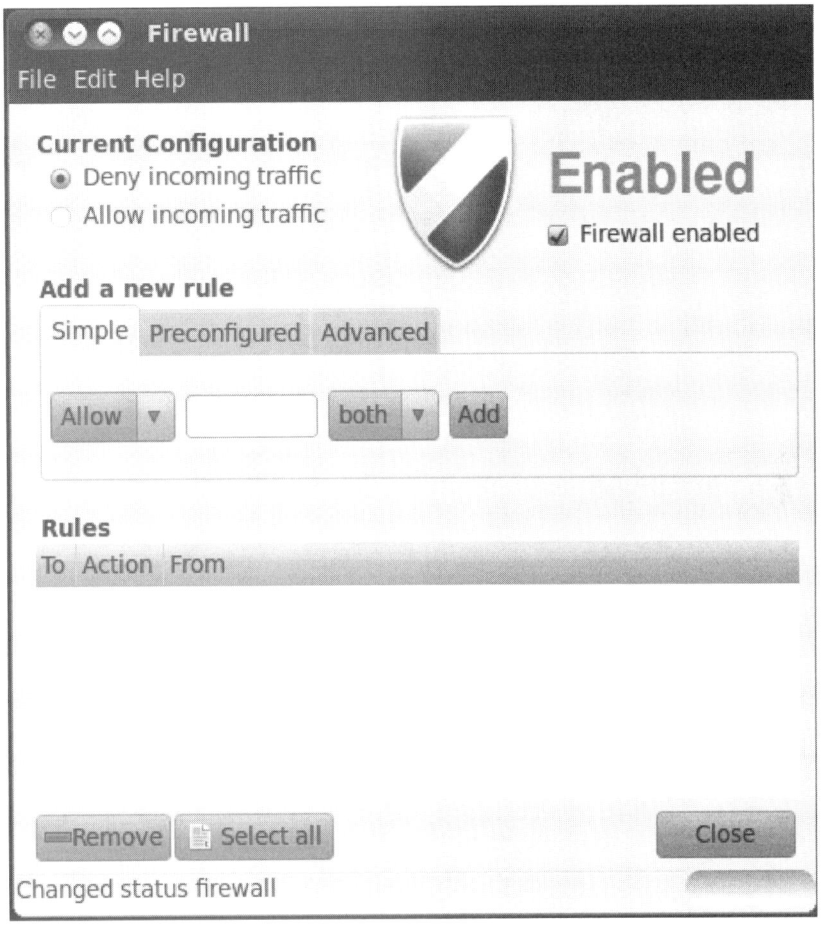

FIGURE 9.4
Enable the firewall

Note:
The next steps use the Gufw tool to configure the internal firewall based on the following predefined policy definition. The focus of this firewall configuration is on denying protocols and services which can be used for port-scanning or file transfer (ICMP [ping], FTP, TFTP, Telnet), and allowing protocols and services commonly used for transactions like Web browsing and e-mail (HTTP/S, SMTP, POP3):

- Deny incoming traffic
- Deny the following protocols: FTP, ICMP, SNMP, Telnet, TFTP
- Allow the following protocols: HTTP, HTTPS POP3, SSH, SMTP

This policy definition will be configured on the firewall by adding rules. Some of the protocols and services can be added using the options on the Preconfigured tab.

15. **Click** the **Preconfigured tab** in the Add a new rule section of the dialog box.
16. **Select Deny** from the **first drop-down menu**.
17. **Select ftp** from the **second drop-down menu** and **click Add** to deny FTP services on the machine. The new rule has been added to the Rules section of the dialog box.

FIGURE 9.5

FTP service denied

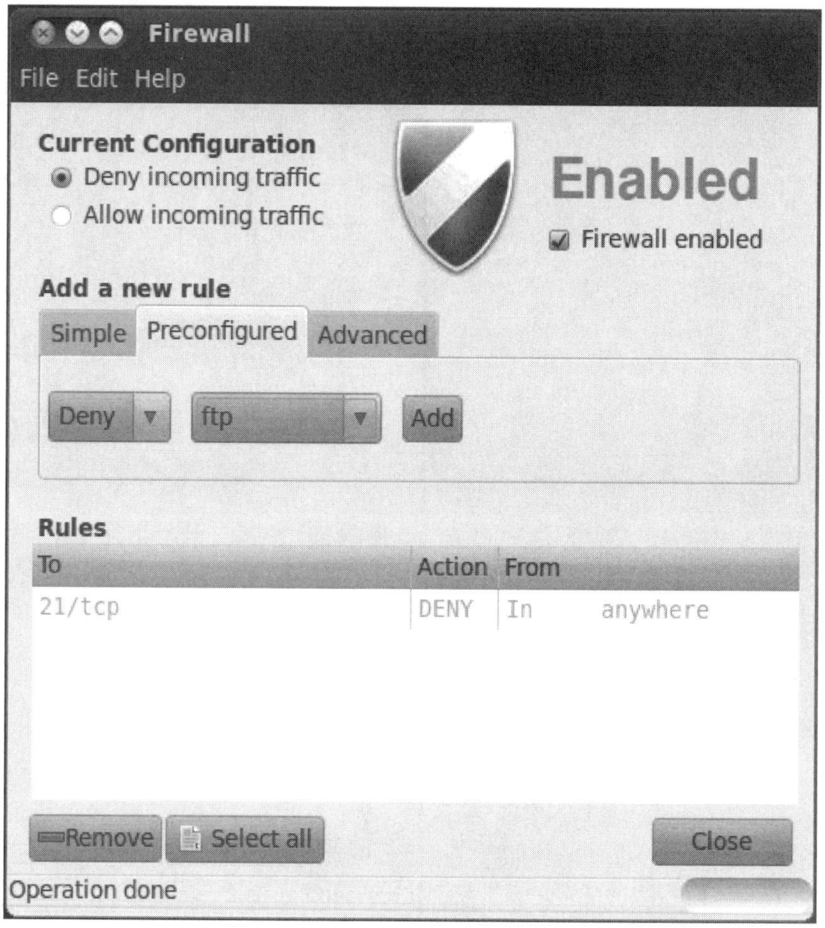

18. **Repeat steps 16-17** to deny the Telnet service.
19. **Select Allow** from the **first drop-down menu**.
20. **Select POP3** from the **second drop-down menu** and **click Add** to allow the POP3 service on the machine. The new rule has been added to the Rules section of the dialog box.
21. **Repeat steps 19-20** to add rules for any other protocols found in the second drop-down menu.

Note:
The Preconfigured tab does not include options for all of the services and protocols that need to be configured. Other rules can be added using the options on the Simple tab; however, the Gufw firewall requires that those services and protocols be entered using their port number and protocol type, as described in the following table.

PROTOCOL OR SERVICE NAME	PORT NUMBER	PROTOCOL TYPE
FTP	20 or 21	TCP
HTTP	80	Both TCP and UDP
HTTPS	443	TCP
ICMP (ping)	7	ICMP is attached to the echo request port, select Both
POP3	110	TCP
SMTP	25	TCP
SNMP	161	UDP
SSH	22	TCP
Telnet	23	TCP
TFTP	69	UDP

22. **Click** the **Simple tab** in the Firewall dialog box.
23. From the first drop-down menu, **select Deny**.
24. Refer to the policy definition described previously, **type 7** (the port number for the ICMP protocol) in the **text box**.
25. **Select both** (as indicated in the table previously) in the **second drop-down menu** and **click Add** to add the rule to the firewall configuration.
26. **Repeat steps 23-25** for the remaining services and protocols found in the policy definition for this lab.
27. **Make a screen capture** of the Firewall window showing all of the rules added during this lab. **Paste** it into a new text document. Be aware that you may have to scroll to see the complete list of rules and that may mean multiple screen captures.

Note:
To capture the screen, **press** the **Ctrl** and **PrtSc** keys together, and then **use Ctrl + V** to paste the image into a Word or other word processor document.

28. **Click** the **Close button** to close the Firewall dialog box.

Note:
The next steps use Gufw (Graphical Uncomplicated Firewall), a GUI interface for the standard Ubuntu Linux Uncomplicated Firewall (ufw) you used in the previous steps. Though the ICMP protocol was denied using the Ubuntu firewall, ping access is hard-coded into the ufw rules definition files. To block ping requests, the before.rules configuration file must be edited using the VI Editor. In the next steps, you will edit the firewall configuration files from the command line prompt.

29. From the Linux toolbar, **click Applications**, **click Accessories**, and **select Terminal** to open the Linux command prompt.
30. At the command line prompt, **type sudo vi /etc/ufw/before.rules** and **press Enter**.
31. If necessary, **type ISS316Security** when prompted for the sudo password.

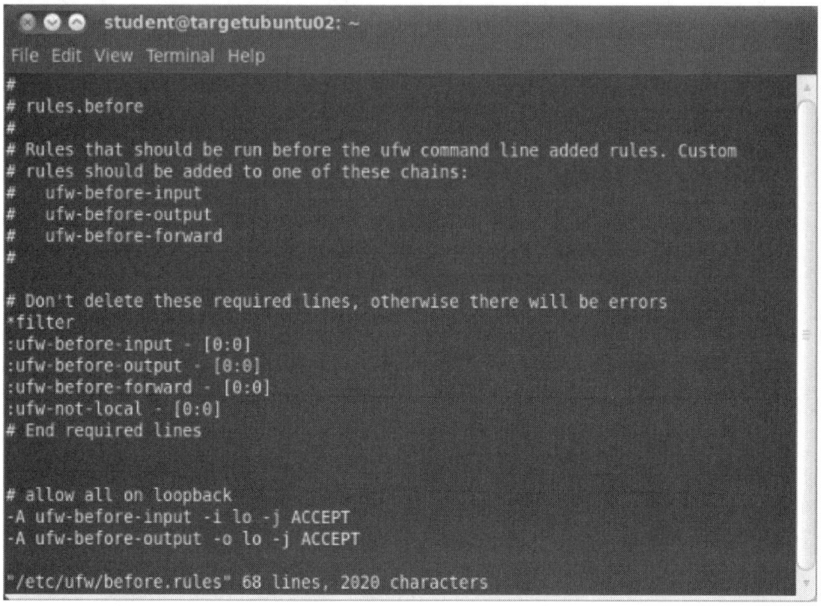

FIGURE 9.6

The /etc/ufw/before.rules rules configuration file

32. Use the arrow keys to **locate** the **–A ufw-before-input –p icmp - -icmp-type echo-request –j ACCEPT** line of code.
33. At the beginning of that line, **press** the **i key** to enter the INSERT mode.
34. **Type #** at the beginning of the line.

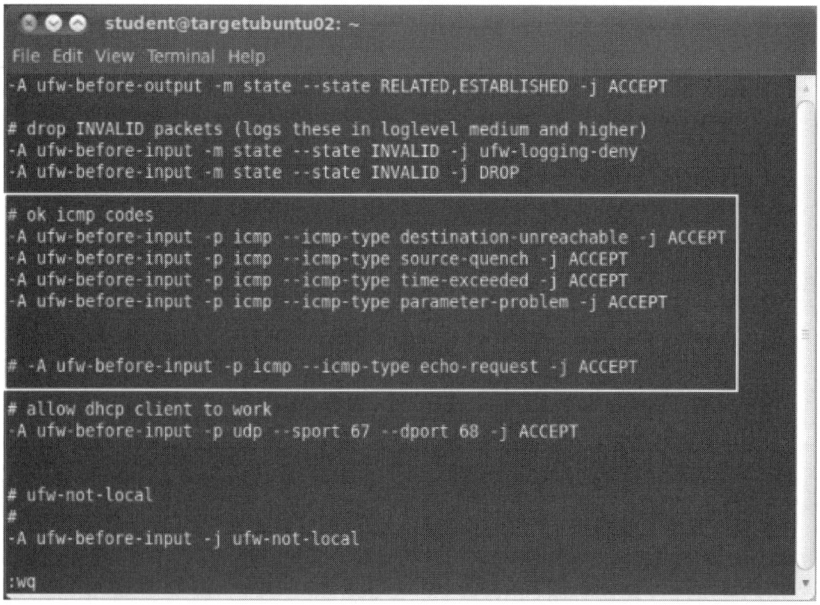

FIGURE 9.7

Editing /etc/ufw/before.rules to disallow ICMP echo requests

35. **Press** the **Esc key** to exit the INSERT mode and **press Shift + :** to return to the command line mode.

    A colon with a blinking cursor at the bottom of the window indicates that you are in the command line mode.
36. **Type wq** to save your changes and exit the VI Editor.
37. **Make a screen capture** of the terminal window showing this change and **paste** it into your text document.
38. Use the **File Transfer button** on the vWorkstation desktop to transfer the document to your physical workstation and submit it to your instructor with your deliverables.
39. **Close** the **TargetUbuntu02 window**.

> **Note:**
> The next steps explore the functionality provided by the Linux-based IP monitoring tools on the TargetUbuntu01 server. The first tool is bmon (a bandwidth monitor).

40. **Maximize** the **TargetUbuntu01 window**.
41. From the Linux toolbar, **click Applications**, **click Accessories**, and **select Terminal** to open the Linux command prompt.
42. In the terminal window, **type bmon** and **press Enter** to access the bandwidth monitor.

    This tool will give you an overview of IP traffic on two interfaces (lo, which stands for local, and eth0 for the IP address). Note that the tool also indicates the packets received (RX rate) and transmitted (TX rate) in bytes.

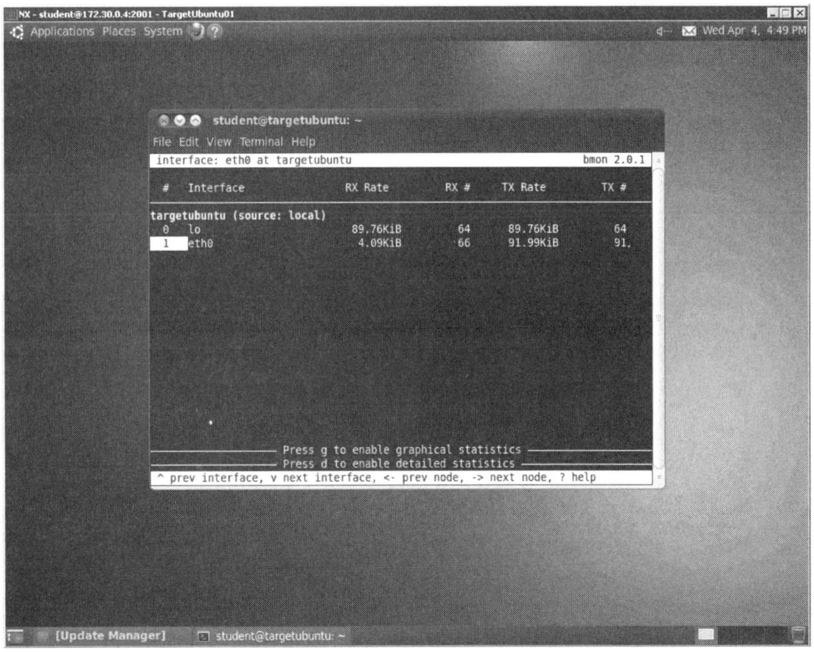

FIGURE 9.8
bmon interfaces

43. **Use** the **arrow keys** to move between the lo and eth0 interfaces. Notice how the transfer rates change.
44. **Type g** to display a real-time graph of the transfer rates. Be aware that you may have to expand the window to see the entire graph. **View** the graph for both interfaces.

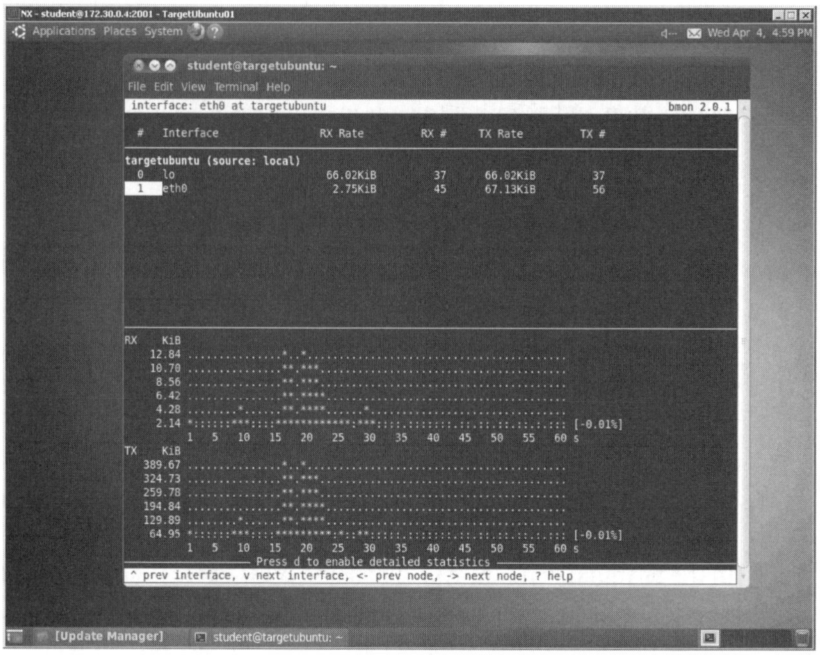

FIGURE 9.9

Graphic view of the bmon interfaces

45. **Type d** to display detailed statistics for both interfaces.

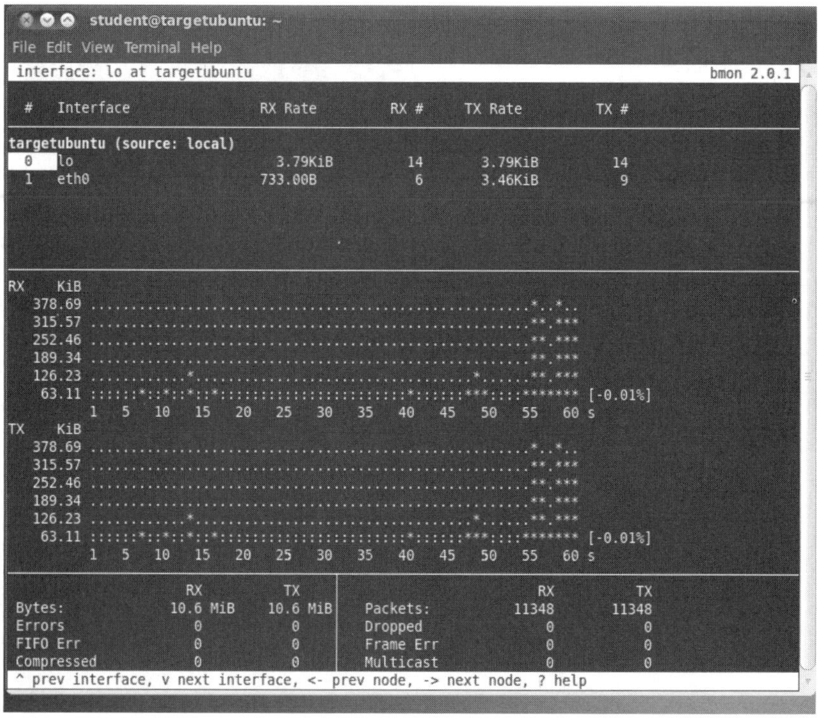

FIGURE 9.10

Detailed statistics from the bmon tool

46. **Make a screen capture** of the bmon window showing the details screen and **paste** it into a new text document.
47. In the bmon window, **type q** to stop the tool. **Type Y** when prompted to confirm that you want to stop the tool.

> **Note:**
> The next steps explore the functionality provided by the iftop tool on the TargetUbuntu01 server. Like bmon, this is a bandwidth monitoring tool.

48. At the command line prompt in the terminal window, **type sudo iftop –i eth0 –F 172.30.0.9 -P** and **press Enter**.
49. **Type ISS316Security** when prompted for a password.

    This command requires root access and uses the sudo command to monitor the eth0 interface on the TargetUbuntu01 server (172.30.0.9) and show the output by host and port name.

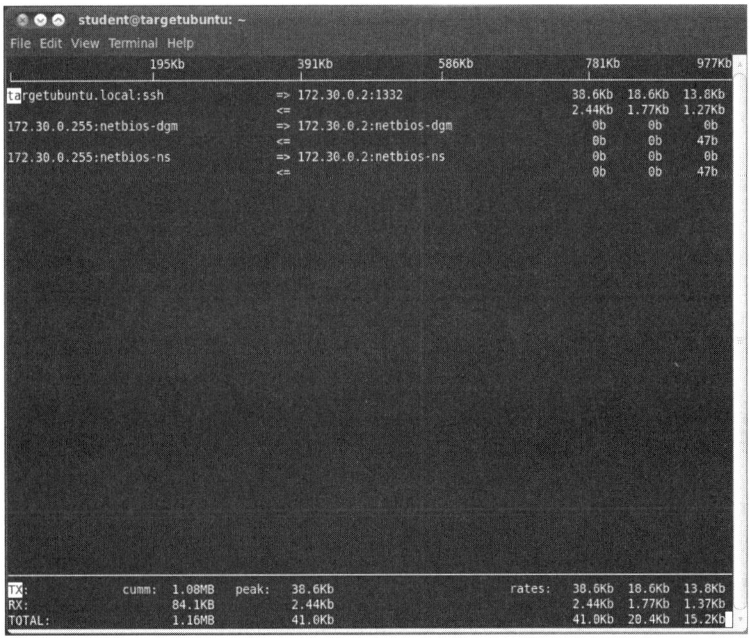

FIGURE 9.11
Output from the iftop tool

50. **Make a screen capture** of the iftop window and **paste** it into your text document.
51. **Type q** to exit iftop.

> **Note:**
> The next steps explore the functionality provided by the pktstat tool on the TargetUbuntu01 server. This bandwidth monitoring tool breaks down usage by protocol type.

52. At the command line prompt, **type sudo pktstat** and **press Enter** to start the tool.
53. **Review** the output for the eth0 interface, **identifying the protocols** that appear.

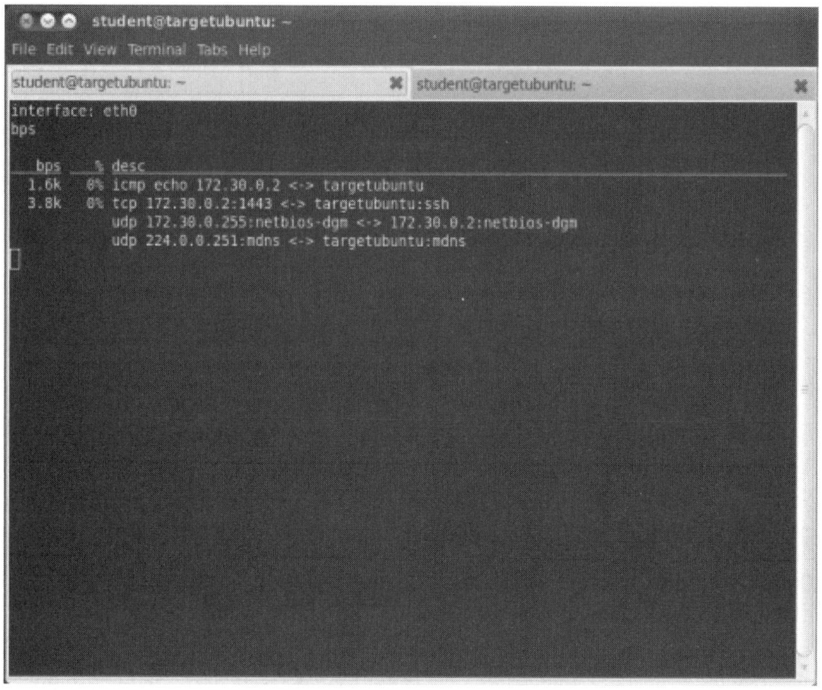

FIGURE 9.12 Output from the pktstat tool

54. **Make a screen capture** of the pktstat window and **paste** it into your text document.
55. **Type q** to exit pktstat.

> **Note:**
> The next steps explore the functionality provided by the iperf tool on the TargetUbuntu01 server. This utility is designed to test the throughput of UDP and TCP packet streams on a network.

56. At the command line prompt, **type iperf –c 172.30.0.4 -u** and **press Enter** to start the tool and determine the UDP bandwidth.

    After a short wait, the window will display the host name and port connection, connection interval time, amount of data transferred, and the bandwidth of the transfer.

57. **Review** the output, **identifying any errors or inconsistencies** that appear.

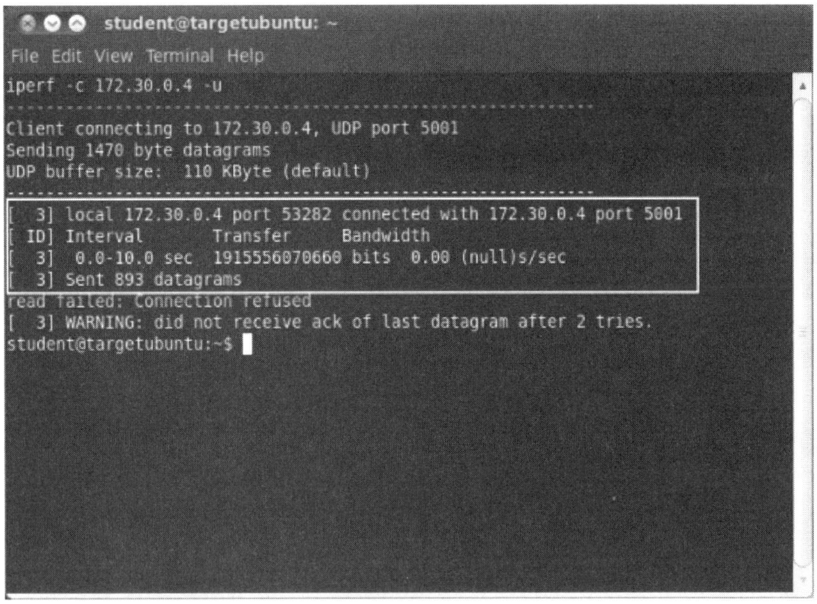

FIGURE 9.13
Output from the iperf tool

58. **Make a screen capture** of the iperf window and **paste** it into your text document.

Note:
The next steps explore the functionality provided by the tcptrack tool on the TargetUbuntu01 server. This utility provides the following information about TCP connections:

- Source and destination port addresses
- Bandwidth used by the connection
- Status of the connection

59. At the command line prompt, **type sudo tcptrack –i eth0** and **press Enter** to start the tool and determine the UDP bandwidth.
60. **Type ISS316Security** when prompted for the sudo password.

    Because no activity has occurred, there is no output in the tcptrack window. The next steps will generate a stream of TCP packets for the tcptrack tool to monitor.

FIGURE 9.14

Output from the tcptrack tool

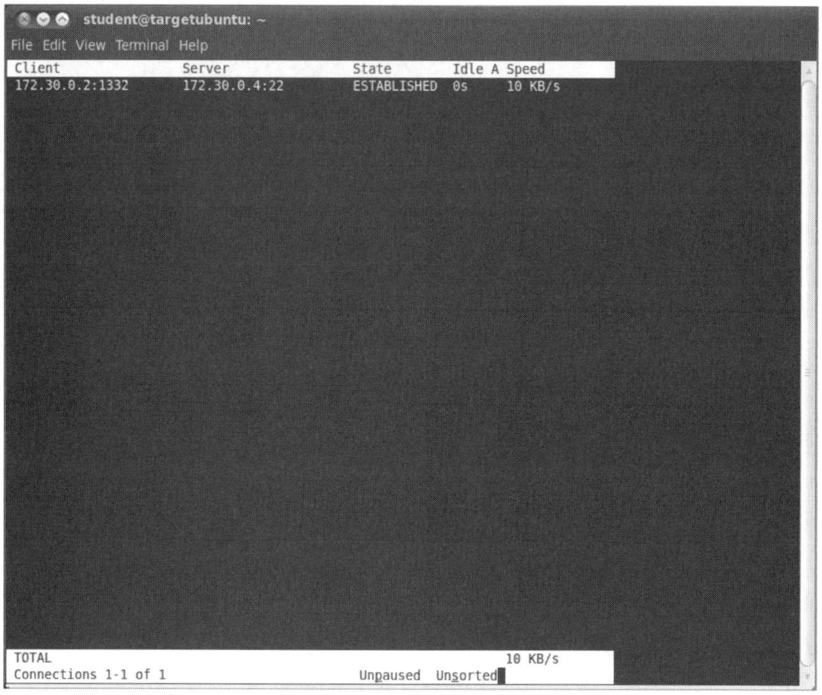

61. On the vWorkstation desktop, **double-click** the **Mozilla Foxfire icon** to start the browser.
62. In the browser's address box, **type http://*inetaddr*/dvwa** and **click Enter** to open the Damn Vulnerable Web Application (DVWA). In place of *inetaddr* use the IP address you documented in step 7 earlier in this lab.
63. **Log in** to the application with the following credentials and **click Login** to continue:
    - Username: **admin**
    - Password: **password**
64. On the DVWA Welcome screen, **click** the **DVWA Security button**.
65. **Select low** from the Script Security drop-down menu. **Click Submit** to change the security level.
66. **Click** the **XSS reflected button** in the DVWA navigation menu.

    XSS vulnerabilities are generally found in Web forms that send and retrieve data to databases via HTML.

67. In the What's your name? box, **type Simon** and **click Submit**.

    The Web form will take the name you entered and repeat it back to you in a friendly welcome.

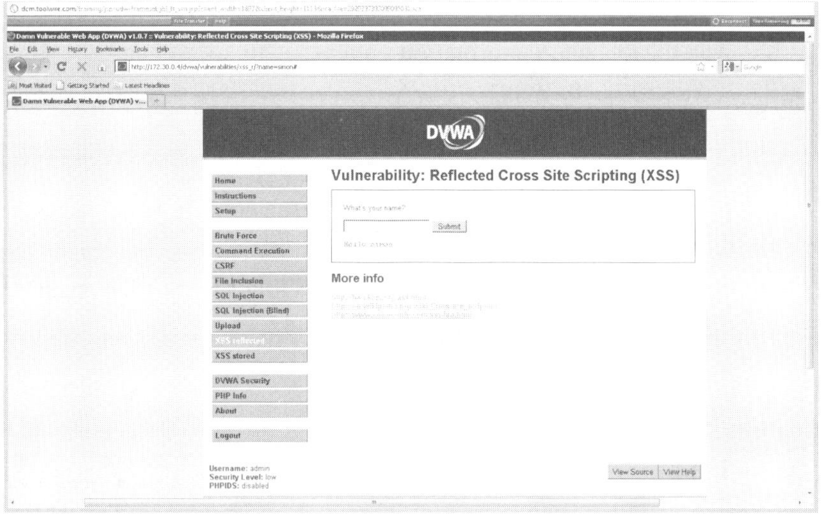

FIGURE 9.15
Output from the XSS test

68. **Repeat step 67** several more times to generate more traffic.
69. **Close** the **Firefox browser** to exit DVWA and make note of any changes to the tcptrack output.
70. **Make a screen capture** of the tcptrack window and **paste** it into your text document.
71. **Close** the **TargetUbuntu01 window**.

> **Note:**
> The next steps help you perform a series of tests using a variety of tools to validate that the firewall settings you established in this lab were configured properly.

72. **Click** the **Windows Start button** on the vWorkstation desktop.
73. **Select Run** from the menu.
74. In the Run dialog box, **type cmd** to open the Windows Command Prompt.
75. At the command prompt, type **ping 172.30.0.9**.

    The replies indicate that the ping attempt was denied.

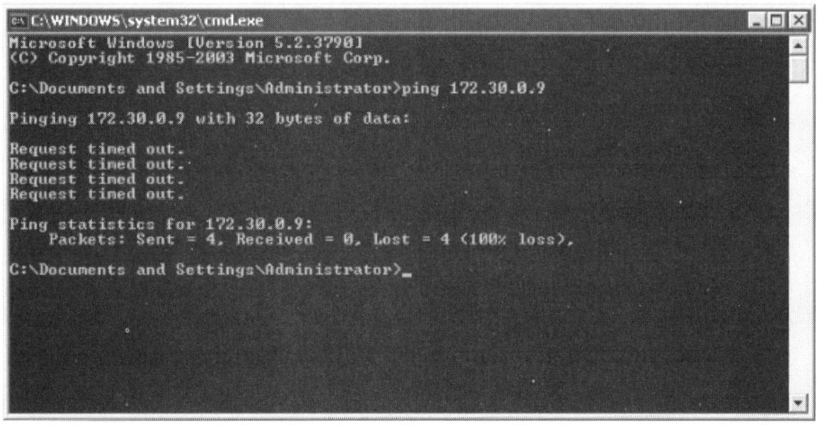

FIGURE 9.16
ping blocked by firewall

76. **Make a screen capture** of the Windows Command Prompt and **paste** it into your text document.
77. **Close** the **Windows Command Prompt**.
78. **Double-click** the **Tftpd32_SE Admin icon** to open the application.
79. **Click** the **Tftp Client tab**.
80. **Type** the following information under the Tftp Client tab:
    - Host: **172.30.0.9**
    - Port: **69**
81. In the Local file section, **click** the **Browse button**.
82. In the Select File dialog box, **navigate** to the **PCAP Test File** and **click Open**.
83. **Click** the **Put button** to start the TFTP file transfer.

    The status response (block #0) indicates that the transfer was not successful and the firewall was configured properly to block this service.

FIGURE 9.17

TFTP transfer blocked by Gufw

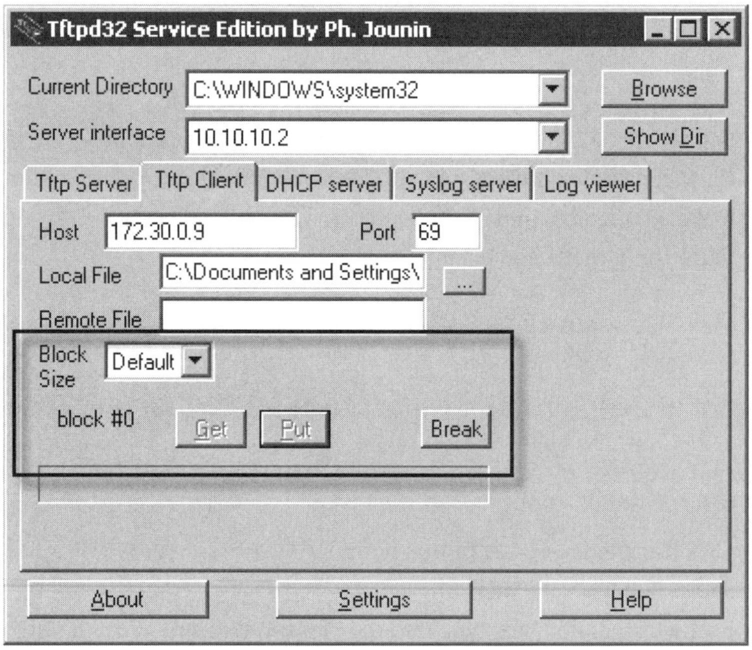

84. **Make a screen capture** of your results and **paste** it into your text document.
85. **Close** the **Tftpd32_SE Admin window**.
86. **Double-click** the **FileZilla icon**.

87. **Type** the following information to log in to the TargetUbuntu02 machine:
    - Host: **172.30.0.9**
    - Username: **student**
    - Password: **ISS316Security**
    - Port: **21**
88. **Click** the **Quickconnect button**.

    The connection timed out trying to connect. This indicates that the FTP service was successfully denied by the firewall configuration.

FIGURE 9.18

FTP connection blocked by Gufw

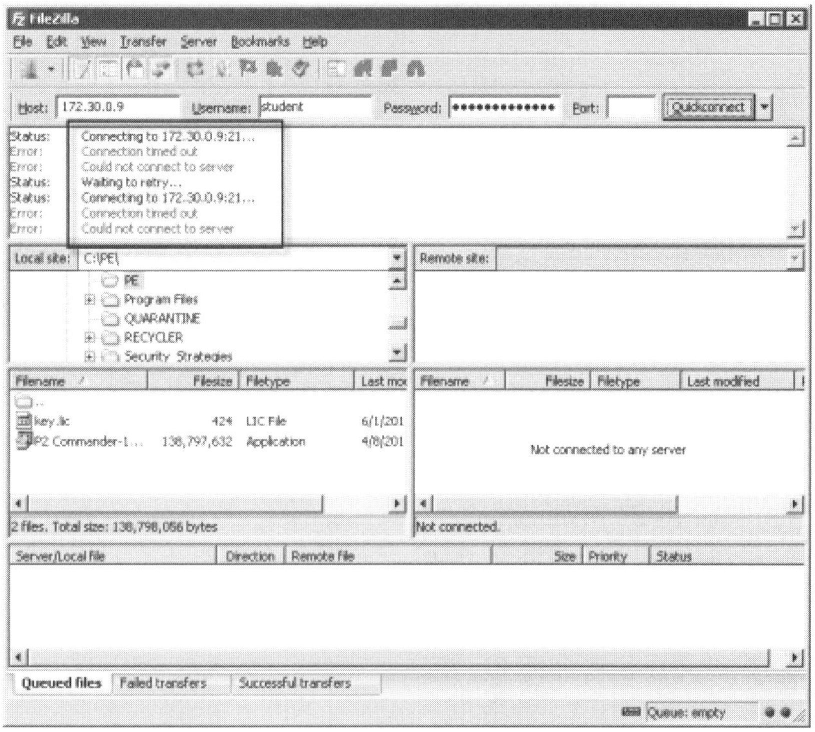

89. **Make a screen capture** of the Filezilla window and **paste** it into your text document.
90. **Close** the **Filezilla window**.
91. **Double-click** the **PuTTY icon** on the desktop to start the PuTTY application.
92. In the PuTTY application window, **type 172.30.0.9** in the Host Name (or IP address) box.
93. **Type 22** in the Port box and **select** the **SSH radio button**. **Click** the **Open button** to start the connection.

94. PuTTY will launch a terminal console window. At the login prompt, **type** the following credentials:
    - User name: **student**
    - Password: **ISS316Security**

    The output indicates that the SSH connection was successfully made indicating that the firewall was properly configured to allow this service.

FIGURE 9.19

SSH access granted by Gufw

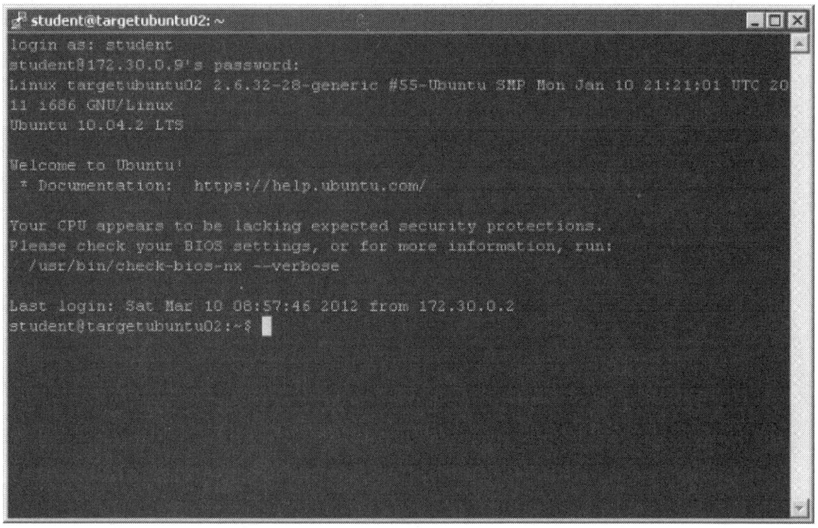

95. **Make a screen capture** of the terminal window and **paste** it into your text document.
96. At the command line prompt, **type quit** to close the terminal window.
97. Use the **File Transfer button** on the vWorkstation desktop to transfer the document to your physical workstation and submit it to your instructor with your deliverables.

Evaluation Criteria and Rubrics

The following are the evaluation criteria and rubrics for Lab #9 that students must perform:

1. Was the student able to list the features and functions of Gufw, an Ubuntu Linux desktop internal host firewall? – [**20%**]
2. Was the student able to document the Ubuntu Linux internal IP stateful firewall with default configuration settings? – [**20%**]
3. Was the student able to configure the Ubuntu Linux internal IP stateful firewall as per policy definition? – [**20%**]
4. Was the student able to monitor IP traffic using applications and tools on a TargetUbuntu server for specific kinds of IP, UDP, or TCP traffic? – [**20%**]
5. Was the student able to test and verify the internal host firewall implementation on the Ubuntu Linux desktop, and monitor IP traffic on a TargetUbuntu server? – [**20%**]

LAB #9 – ASSESSMENT SPREADSHEET

Construct a Linux Host Firewall and Monitor for IP Traffic

Course Name and Number: ______________________________

Student Name: ______________________________

Instructor Name: ______________________________

Lab Due Date: ______________________________

Internal Firewall Policy Definition

Configure your "TargetUbuntu02" desktop Linux internal host IP stateful firewall according to the following policy definition. Test and validate your implementation after you configure it based on the policy definition. The following is your Ubuntu internal firewall policy definition:

- Deny incoming traffic
- Deny the following specific applications:
  - TFTP
  - Telnet
  - SNMP
  - ICMP
  - FTP
- Allow the following specific applications under "Advanced" settings:
  - SSH
  - SMTP
  - POP3
  - HTTPS
  - HTTP

Make a screen capture of the changes you made to the configuration and paste it into the text document. Use the File Transfer button to download the text file to your local computer and submit it as part of your deliverables.

LAB #9 – ASSESSMENT WORKSHEET

Construct a Linux Host Firewall and Monitor for IP Traffic

Course Name and Number: ______________________________

Student Name: ______________________________

Instructor Name: ______________________________

Lab Due Date: ______________________________

Overview

In this lab, you configured the Gufw Ubuntu host IP stateful firewall as an internal service running on the Linux desktop. By defining what IP traffic is allowed and what IP traffic is denied, you implemented another layer of security in your overall layered security strategy. In addition, you explored some useful network management and security operation tools, which can be enabled to monitor your IP traffic and security functions.

Lab Assessment Questions & Answers

1. Briefly explain how the Gufw internal Ubuntu host IP stateful firewall can be used in a layered security strategy at the workstation domain level.

____

____

____

____

2. Briefly explain how each of the Linux-based tools demonstrated in this lab can be used to monitor bandwidth, protocol, and network traffic information.

____

____

____

____

____

3. Given that the Ubuntu internal firewall is not installed by default, should you enable this firewall if your organization already has a firewall at your LAN-to-WAN domain's Internet ingress/egress point? Why or why not?

4. How do you block specific ports and IP ranges from communicating via TCP/IP to and from your Ubuntu Target VM using Gufw?

5. Other than Deny or Allow incoming connections, what other options are available in Ubuntu's internal firewall? Why would they include any additional option?

6. What usefulness is there in monitoring IP traffic to and from an individual workstation or server?

7. Explain both the information systems security practitioner and hacker perspectives of using a security scanning application against a protected or unprotected host.

8. How are you going to test if your internal firewall configuration is working properly?

9. Define a test plan to test, verify, and monitor traffic on your internal Ubuntu Target VM.

10. This is a two–part, real-world scenario question. Read the REQUIREMENTS section. Then, based on the requirements, answer PART A with a technical solution using the tools demonstrated in this lab and answer PART B with a written explanation and justification for your solution.

You must use at least two of the following Linux-based IP monitor tools presented in this lab in your real-world example: bmon, iftop, pktstat, iperf, and/or tcptrack.

REQUIREMENTS: A strategy is required to effectively monitor IP traffic on an individual server as well as many servers on a "point in time" as well as on an "over time" basis. There is also a requirement to automate the alerting of potential issues based on changes in network utilization.

PART A: Give a real-world example of how you could meet this requirement with the use of tools presented in this lab and the use of any other available resources, such as scripts, alerts, output formats, or scheduled tasks (i.e., cron jobs).

PART B: Explain the usefulness and benefits of your real-world example to an organization and support your reasoning with technical facts and security in mind. Did you meet the requirements? Why or why not?

Design and Implement Security Operations Management Best Practices

LAB 10

Introduction

In this lab, you will use the Splunk administration tool to develop a standard operating procedure for implementing security operations best practices. After exploring the main areas of Splunk, you will use it to create a security monitoring and alerting solution. You will also work alone or in a small group to organize and prioritize the information about network, IT, and security assets into a security operations management best practices deliverable based on your work in Lab #6 and Lab #8.

Learning Objectives

Upon completing this lab, you will be able to:

- Organize necessary device, system, and application information needed to implement a security operations management best practices procedure
- Prioritize network- and host-based assets that require monitoring for the secure operations of the Cisco Mock IT infrastructure and VM server farm
- Design a security monitoring solution using Splunk while aligning the strategy to industry best practices for security monitoring and log management
- Create a standard operating procedure (SOP) document that describes the implementation of the security operations management best practices strategy used for this infrastructure

TOOLS AND SOFTWARE USED

NAME	MORE INFORMATION
Splunk	http://www.splunk.com

Deliverables

Upon completion of this lab, you are required to provide the following deliverables to your instructor, as a team:

1. A security operations management best practices document based on the Cisco Mock IT infrastructure;
2. Review Lab #6 and Lab #8 deliverables and create a document explaining your rationale for why a security monitoring and operations management strategy is critical;
3. A CSV version of one of the Splunk preconfigured searches;
4. Lab Assessment Questions & Answers for Lab #10.

Note:
Completion of Lab #6 and Lab #8 is *not required* to complete this lab. If you did not perform Lab #6 and Lab #8, you may skip deliverable #2. If you are unsure whether this deliverable is required for your course, please consult your instructor.

Hands-On Steps

1. This lab begins at the student landing vWorkstation virtual machine desktop of the VSCL, as shown here.

FIGURE 10.1

"Student Landing" VSCL workstation

Note:

The next steps open the Splunk administration tool and change the logon password. Splunk is a cloud-based collection of applications that perform a very thorough collection and analysis of data from a variety of machine sources. You will access Splunk via an Internet browser and explore its core applications: Index Data, Search & Investigate, Add Knowledge, Monitor & Alert, and Report & Analyze. Identify which functions can help in monitoring security operations in the lab. You will need this information for the deliverables in this lab.

2. **Double-click** on the **Firefox icon** on the vWorkstation desktop.

   You can access Splunk from any Internet browser, but the instructions in this lab use Firefox.
3. In the browser's address box, **type http://127.0.0.1:8000** (the URL for Splunk).

   The system will attempt to check for updates by connecting with Splunk.com; however, the virtual Workstation does not have access to the Internet, so **click Continue** to proceed.
4. If prompted, log on to Splunk using the following credentials (they are also shown on the logon page itself):
   - Username: **admin**
   - Password: **changeme**

   If you are not prompted to change your password, proceed to step 6.
5. Follow the online instructions for changing your password using the following credentials and **click Save Password** to continue:
   - NewPassword: **ISS316Security**
   - Confirm NewPassword: **ISS316Security**
6. At the Splunk Welcome screen, **click** the **Splunk Home tab** in the toolbar.

7. On the Splunk Home page, **click** the **Getting started link**.

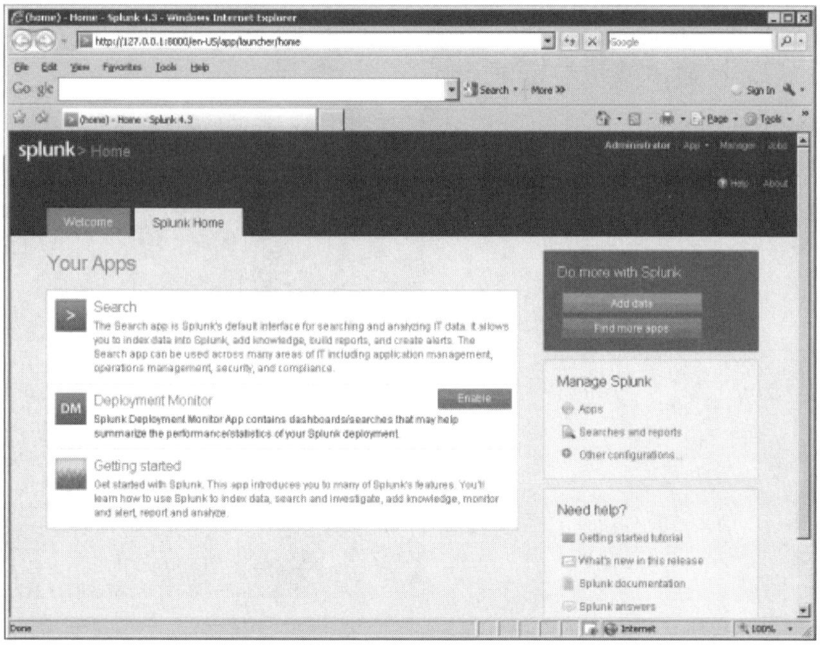

FIGURE 10.2
Splunk Home screen

8. From the Getting started page, **click** on the **Index Data tab**. **Review** the information found on the screen.

   The first step in configuring Splunk for analysis uses the Index Data tool, which allows Splunk to index the data from any computer in your infrastructure.

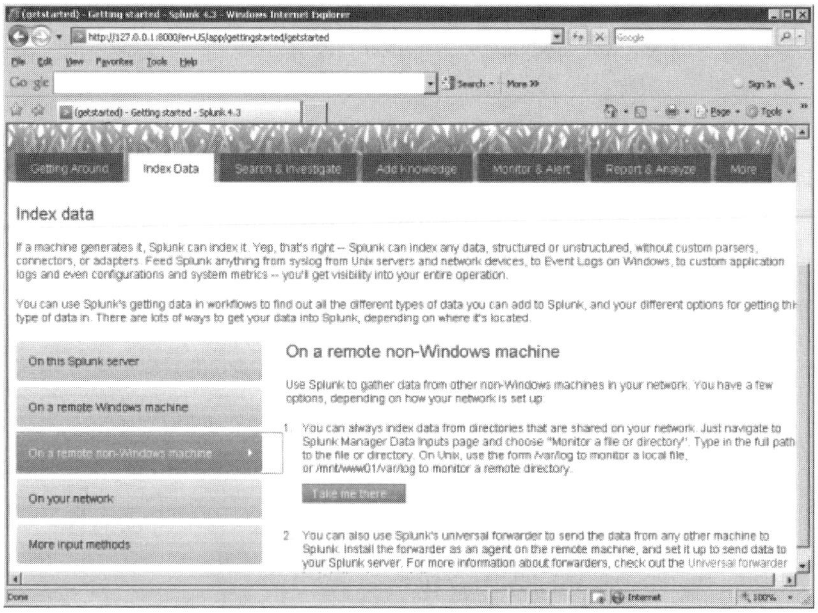

FIGURE 10.3
Index Data tab

9. **Click** the **Search & Investigate tab** on the Splunk navigation bar. **Review** the information found on the screen.

   Once data is loaded into Splunk, it can be searched by a variety of methods, which are listed on the tabs on the left-hand side.

10. **Click** the **Add Knowledge tab** on the Splunk navigation bar. **Review** the information found on the screen.

    This tool enables you to add context to your data by naming fields and data points.

11. **Click** the **Monitor & Alert tab** on the Splunk navigation bar. **Review** the information found on the screen.

    This feature allows you to set up searches, configure alerts, and monitor your infrastructure for specific events. **Click** the **Set up an alert button** on the left and review the information on that screen. You will use this information as part of your deliverables for this lab.

12. **Click** the **Report & Analyze tab** on the Splunk navigation bar. **Review** the information found on the screen.

    The Report Builder enables you to create and schedule ongoing reports and to define and format sophisticated charts.

13. **Click** the **Manager link** in the top navigation bar.

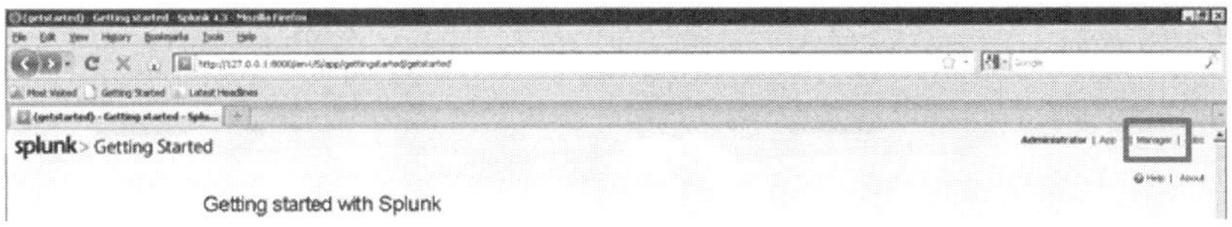

FIGURE 10.4
Linking to the Splunk Manager

14. **Review** the information found on the screen. The Splunk Manager tool is the central interface for all of the commonly used features and functions of Splunk.

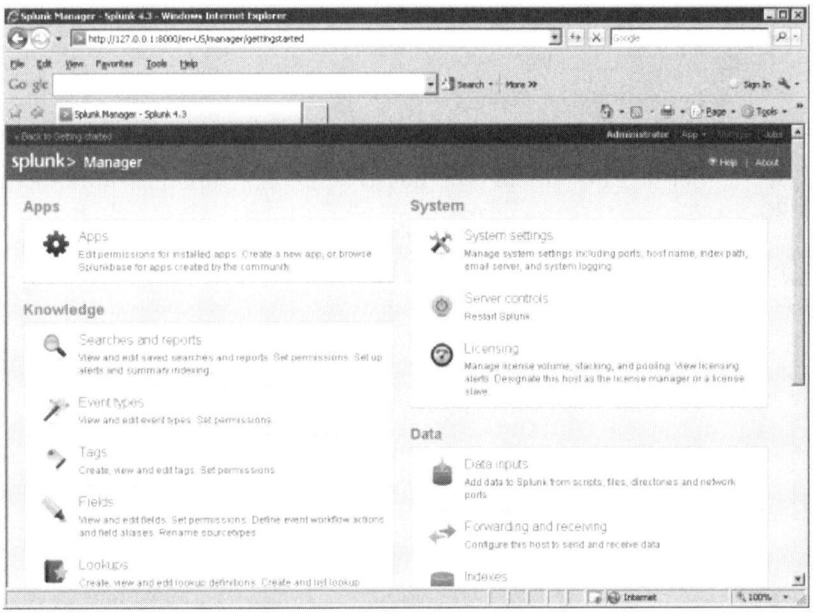

FIGURE 10.5
Splunk Manager home screen

> **Note:**
> The next steps use the Splunk tool to load data from the virtual lab, run a search, and save the results of that search. The first step in this process is to input data from the lab into Splunk.

15. **Click Data inputs** under the Data heading on the Manager screen.
16. **Click** the **Add Data button** at the top of the screen.
17. **Click** the **From a TCP port link** under the Or Choose a Data Source header in the lower half of the screen.

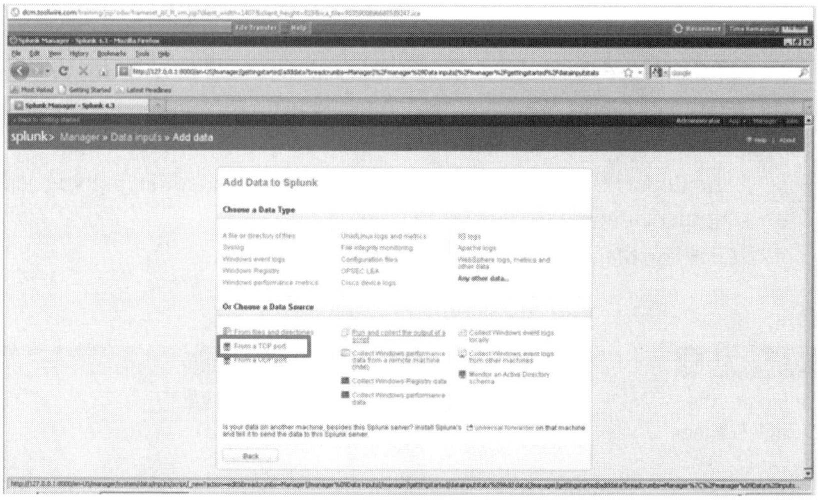

FIGURE 10.6

The Add Data to Splunk screen

18. In the Add Data screen, **type or select** the following information:

    Source heading:
    - TCP port: **22**
    - Accept connections from all hosts?: **No, restrict to one host**
    - Host Restriction: **172.30.0.2**

    Source type heading:
    - Set sourcetype: **Manual**
    - Source type: **tcp-raw**
19. **Click** the **More settings checkbox** to reveal more options, and **click** the **IP radio button** when it appears.

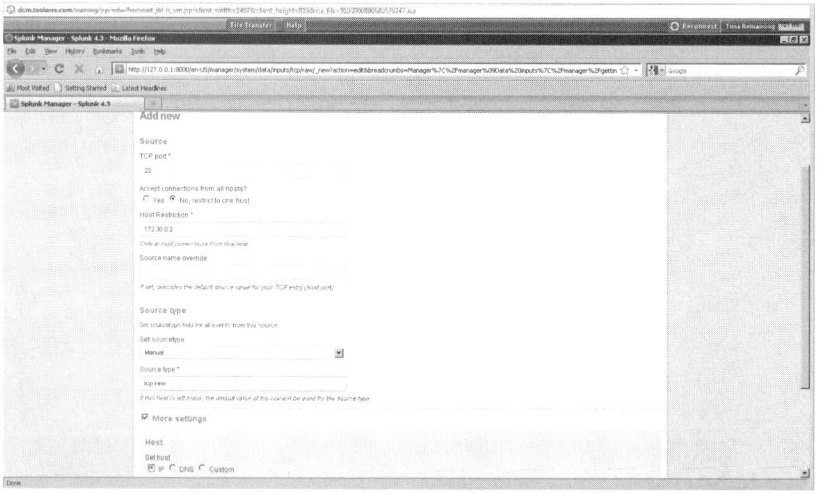

FIGURE 10.7

Adding data parameters

20. **Click** the **Save button** to let Splunk index your data.

    Splunk will display a success message when the new data source has been added.

21. On the Success screen, **click** the **Data inputs link** to return to the Data inputs configuration page.

FIGURE 10.8

Success message

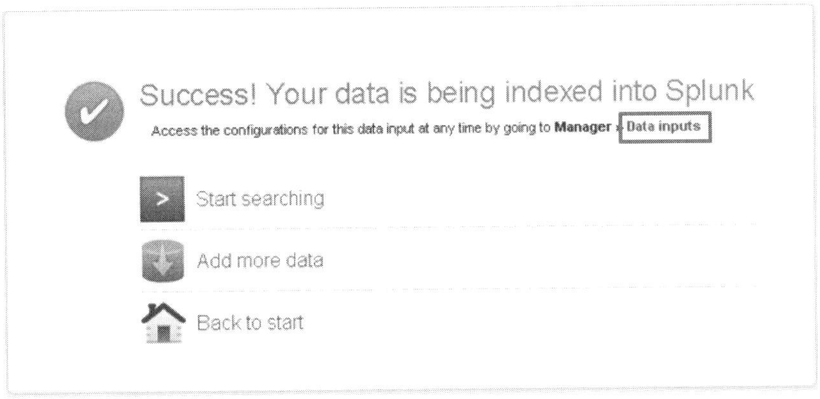

22. **Click** the **TCP link** to return to the TCP configuration page.

FIGURE 10.9

Successful addition of data input

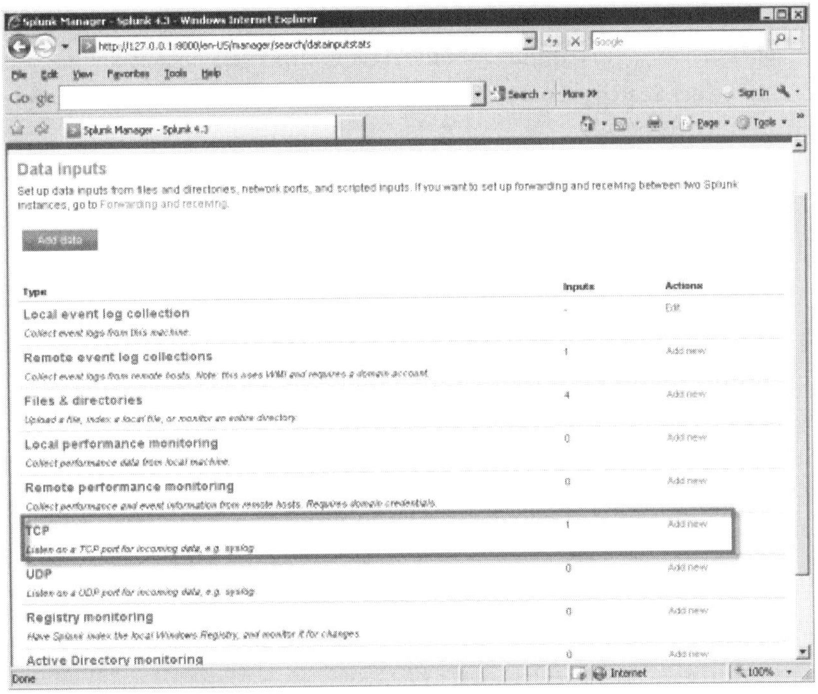

23. **Verify** that the data you input into Splunk (from TCP port 172.30.0.2) appears on the TCP page, and **click** the **Manager link** at the top of the page to return to the Manager tool.

FIGURE 10.10

TCP port data input line item

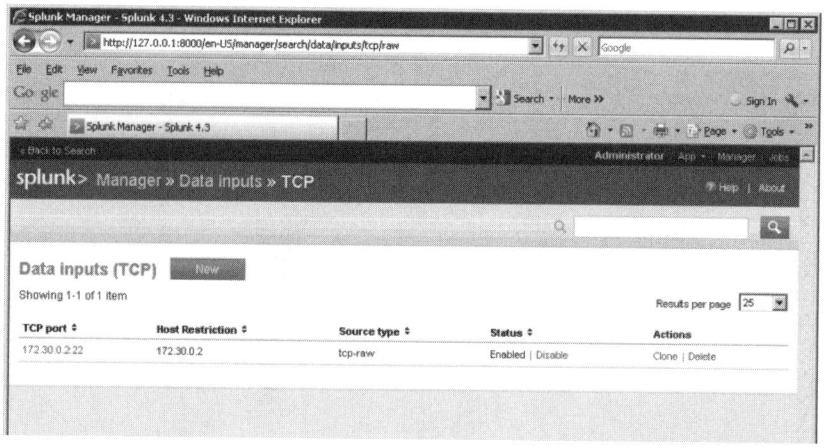

> **Note:**
> The next steps use the Splunk tool to search the data you just loaded into the tool.

24. On the Splunk Manager home screen, **click** the **Searches and reports link** under the Knowledge heading.
25. **Select Search (search)** from the **App context drop-down menu** at the top of the Searches and reports page.
26. **Click** the **Top five sourcetypes** search name.

    The application displays the search string for this report.
27. **Make note** of the search string. You will need it as a deliverable for this lab.
28. **Click Cancel** to return to the Searches and reports homepage.
29. **Click Run** under the Actions heading for the *Top five sourcetypes* search item.

FIGURE 10.11

Searches and reports page

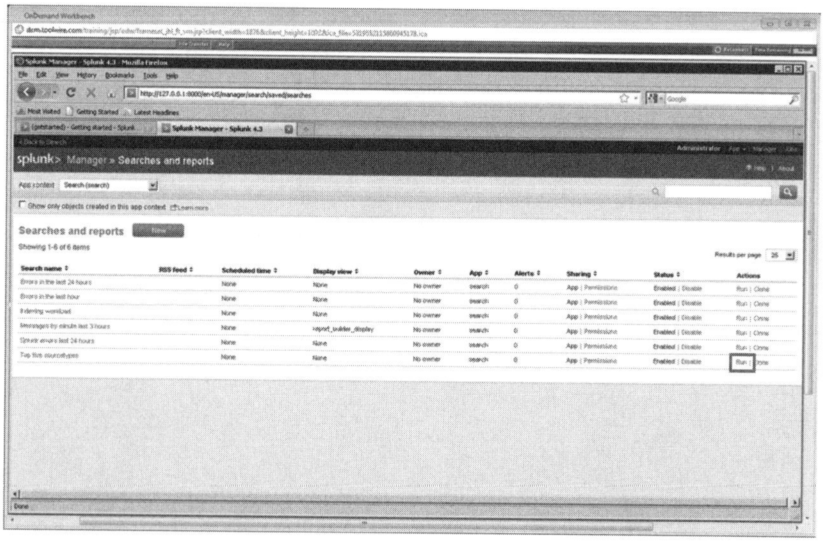

30. **Review** the results of this search.

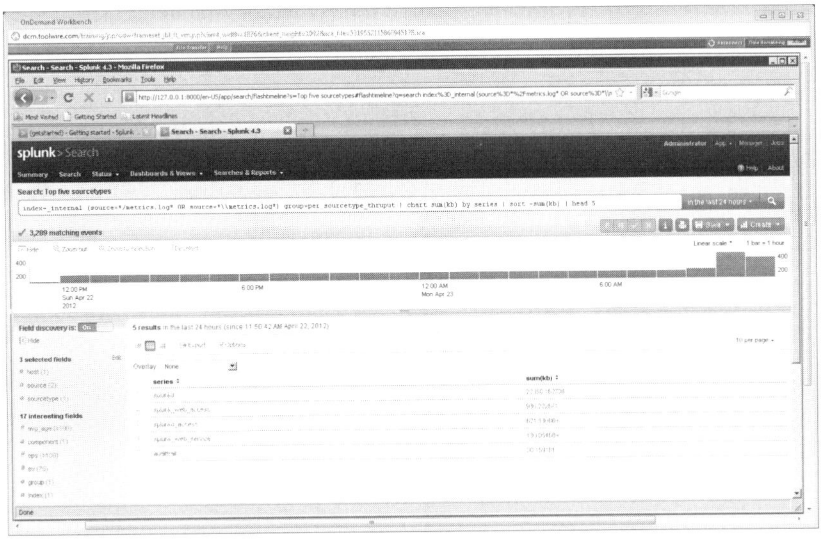

FIGURE 10.12

Results of the Top five sourcetypes search

31. **Click** the **chart icon** directly above the results list to see the results in the form of a column chart instead of a list.

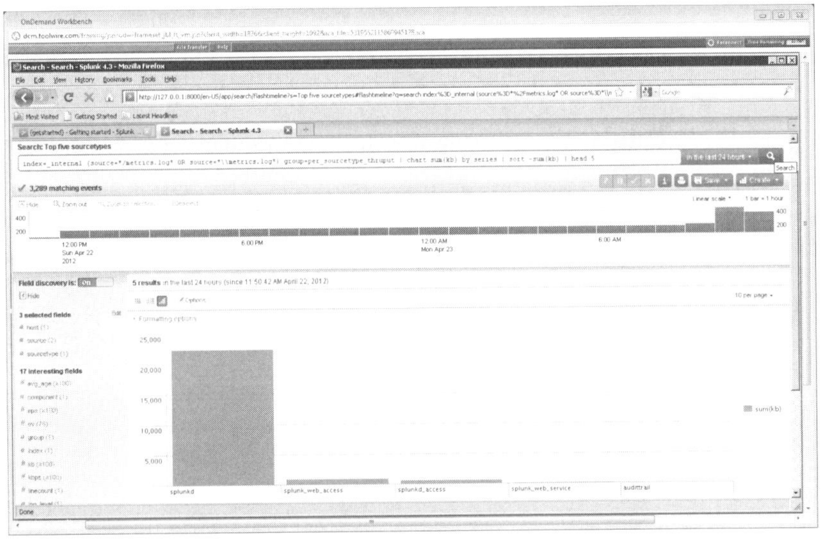

FIGURE 10.13

Charted version of the Top five sourcetypes search

32. **Click** the **Formatting options link** above the chart.

    The tool displays options for changing the chart type, adding a title, and more. **Make note** of the chart types available; you will need this information as part of your deliverables for this lab.

33. In the Chart title box, **type Lab10 Top Five Sourcetypes** to add a title to the chart.

    Review the changes this makes to your display.

34. In the Legend placement drop-down, **select Bottom** to move the legend to the bottom of the chart. Review the changes this makes to your display.

35. **Click** the **bullets icon** to return to the listed version of the search results.

36. **Click** the **Exports icon** directly above the listed results.
    The Export Results dialog box opens.
37. In the File name box, **type Lab10 Top Five Sourcetypes**.
38. **Select CSV** from the Format drop-down menu, if necessary, and **click Export**.

FIGURE 10.14

Exporting the Top five sourcetypes search

39. In the Opening Lab10 Top Five Sourcetypes.csv dialog box, **click OK** to download the file.
40. **Double-click** the **Lab10 Top Five Sourcetypes.csv link** in the Downloads window to open the report in the Notepad.

FIGURE 10.15

Downloading the Top five sourcetypes search

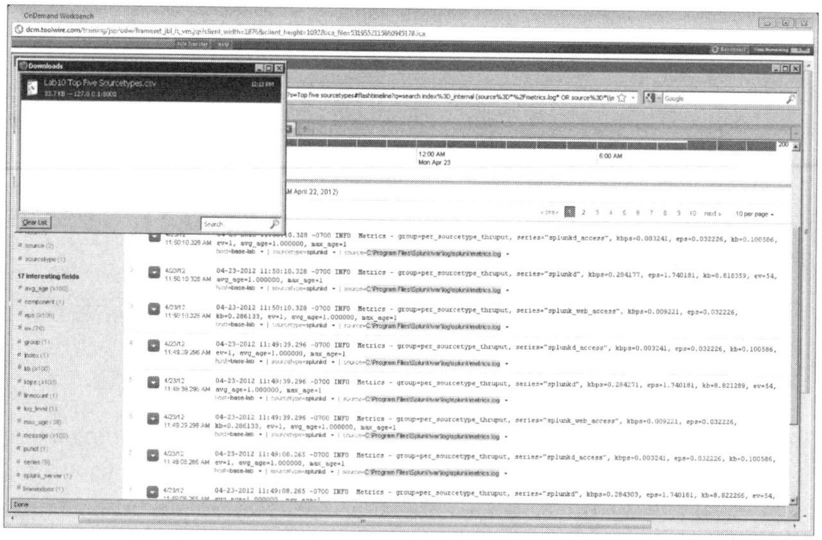

FIGURE 10.16

Opening the Top Five sourcetypes search report

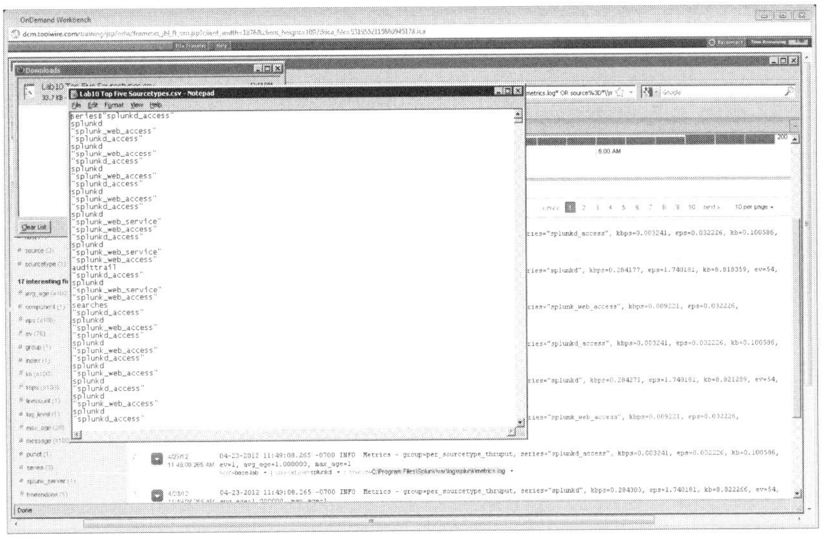

41. From the Notepad menu, **select File > Save As**.
42. In the Save As dialog box, **click** the **Desktop button** and **click Save** to save the report to the vWorkstation desktop.
43. **Close the Firefox browser** to end the Splunk session.
44. Use the **File Transfer button** to download the **csv file** to your local computer and submit it as part of your deliverables.

Evaluation Criteria and Rubrics

The following are the evaluation criteria and rubrics for Lab #10 that the students must perform:

1. Was the student able to organize necessary device, system, and application information needed to implement a security operations management best practices procedure? – **[25%]**
2. Was the student able to prioritize network- and host-based assets that require monitoring for the secure operations of the Cisco Mock IT infrastructure and VM server farm? – **[25%]**
3. Was the student able to design a security monitoring solution using Splunk while aligning the strategy to industry best practices for security monitoring and log management? – **[25%]**
4. Was the student able to create a standard operating procedure (SOP) document that describes the implementation of the security operations management best practices strategy used for this infrastructure? – **[25%]**

LAB #10 – ASSESSMENT WORKSHEET A

Design and Implement Security Operations Management Best Practices

Course Name and Number: ______________________________

Student Name: ______________________________

Instructor Name: ______________________________

Lab Due Date: ______________________________

Overview

Review the deliverables you created for Lab #6 and Lab #8, including the following:

From Lab #6:

- Block diagram of a LAN-to-WAN DMZ in Microsoft® PowerPoint, Visio, or OpenOffice;
- Functional overview document explaining your DMZ and LAN-to-WAN security solution;
- Your answers to the Lab #6 Assessment Questions and Answers.

From Lab #8:

- Block diagram design of the Mock IT infrastructure components in Microsoft® PowerPoint or Visio;
- Functional overview document explaining each of the security controls and security countermeasures enabled within each block/component;
- Your answers to the Lab #8 Assessment Questions and Answers.

Security Monitoring and Operations Management Rationale

Using the information just reviewed as the basis for your answer, develop a short text document (no more than two pages) detailing your rationale for why a security monitoring and operations management strategy is critical.

Note:
To successfully complete this deliverable, you will need access to a text editor or word processor, such as Word. If you don't have a word processor or graphics package, use OpenOffice on the student landing vWorkstation for your lab deliverables and to answer the lab assessment questions. To capture screenshots, **press Prt Sc > MSPAINT, paste** into a text document, and **save** the document in the Security_Strategies folder (**C:\Security_Strategies**) using the File Transfer function.

LAB #10 – ASSESSMENT WORKSHEET B

Design and Implement Security Operations Management Best Practices

Course Name and Number: ______________________

Student Name: ______________________

Instructor Name: ______________________

Lab Due Date: ______________________

Overview

Work alone or in a small group and formulate a strategy for implementing a security operations management best practices policy for the Cisco Mock IT infrastructure. Reference the deliverables you submitted for Lab #6 and Lab #8 as part of your discussion. Answer the following questions and indicate, where possible, how tools like Splunk contribute to the overall strategy you develop. Record your strategy in a text document of no longer than five pages and provide it to your instructor as a deliverable for this lab.

> **Note:**
> To successfully complete this deliverable, you will need access to a text editor or word processor, such as Word. If you don't have a word processor or graphics package, use OpenOffice on the student landing vWorkstation for your lab deliverables and to answer the lab assessment questions. To capture screenshots, **press Prt Sc > MSPAINT, paste** into a text document, and **save** the document in the Security_Strategies folder (**C:\Security_Strategies**) using the File Transfer function.

Network/Security Assessment Questionnaire

Network Assessment – Required Information

1. Do you have detailed logical network drawings? If so, please attach.

____

____

____

____

2. What Directory service, if any, is in use?

3. How many network elements do you have? List each, including make and model or attach list.

4. Have you configured multiple networks on this infrastructure?

5. What internal (RFC1918 or otherwise not-Internet-routable) IP address ranges do you use?

6. What external (Internet routable) address ranges do you use?

7. What protocols are in use on your network?

8. What is the role of each network? (Attach list if multiple networks.)

9. How many hosts do you have on the network?

10. What operating systems are used among your servers and workstations?

11. What applications rely on your network(s)?

12. How many Internet-exposed servers are on your network?

13. What applications do you use to manage your network(s)?

14. What geographic locations connect to your network(s)?

15. What are your future growth plans for your network(s)?

Security Assessment – Required Information

1. Do you have firewalls, ACLs, or other types of traffic filters in place within your network? If yes, please describe.

2. What is the general firewall policy: Default permit, default deny inbound, default permit outbound?

3. Do you have any other filtering technologies implemented at the network or host level, such as data leakage prevention, spam filtering, and Web application firewall or other? If so, please describe.

4. Do you use wireless networking? If so, what types? What wireless security measures are in place?

5. Do you use any of the following technologies, and if so, what model:

   a. IDS/IPS: ____________________

   b. Antivirus: ____________________

   c. Anti-spyware or anti-spam: ____________________

   d. Desktop encryption: ____________________

   e. Other: ____________________

6. Do you use VPNs to connect? If so, what type and vendor of VPN software do you use?

7. What services are permitted inbound to your network? Such as SMTP, DNS, HTTP, FTP, or other?

8. Are the servers delivering these services in a DMZ?

9. Are your various system logs aggregated to a central location for monitoring and analysis?

10. Do you have a patch management system in place? If so, please describe.

LAB #10 – ASSESSMENT WORKSHEET C

Design and Implement Security Operations Management Best Practices

Course Name and Number: ______________________________

Student Name: ______________________________

Instructor Name: ______________________________

Lab Due Date: ______________________________

Overview

This lab presented the process of how to design and implement security operations management best practices. You used Splunk to demonstrate how to gather all the information necessary to implement a security operations management best practices solution. This lab thoroughly evaluated your knowledge of the infrastructure worked on and built throughout the course as well as your capability to bring it all together.

Lab Assessment Questions & Answers

1. During the lab demo, how did you connect to the Splunk management tool?

____

____

____

____

2. What are the main functions of Splunk that were demonstrated in the lab and why do they help build more secure operations?

____

____

____

____

____

3. What types of "Data Inputs" are available in Splunk and most other log management tools?

4. What types of "Alert Conditions" are available in Splunk and most other log management tools?

5. What is the search string for the "Top five sourcetypes" preconfigured Search?

6. Describe at least three examples of security- or operations-related Windows Management Reports and Searches that are preconfigured and available within Splunk.

7. What Chart Types are available for a search or report within Splunk?

8. Based on the information you learned in the Getting started module of Splunk, which preconfigured search would you wish to receive via the Alerts feature described? Explain the reasoning behind scheduling this particular alert. How will this alert help your goal of implementing security operations management best practices?